Film and Television Acting

Second Edition

Film and Television Acting
From Stage to Screen

Second Edition

Ian Bernard

Focal Press

An Imprint of Elsevier

Boston   Oxford   Johannesburg   Melbourne   New Delhi   Singapore

Butterworth–Heinemann is an imprint of Elsevier

 Recognizing the importance of preserving what has been written, Elsevier
prints its books on acid-free paper whenever possible.

 Elsevier supports the efforts of American Forests and the Global
ReLeaf program in its campaign for the betterment of trees, forests, and our
environment.

Library of Congress Cataloging-in-Publication Data
Bernard, Ian (Ian J.), 1930–
    Film and television acting : from stage to screen / Ian Bernard.—2nd ed.
        p.   cm.
    Includes index.
    ISBN-13: 978-0-240-80301-2   ISBN-10: 0-240-80301-9 (paperback: alk. paper)
    1. Motion picture acting.   2. Acting for television.   I. Title.
PN1995.9.A26B47   1997
791.43'028—dc21   97-24630
ISBN-13: 978-0-240-80301-2   CIP
ISBN-10: 0-240-80301-9
British Library Cataloguing-in-Publication Data
A catalogue record for this book is available from the British Library.

The publisher offers special discounts on bulk orders of this book.
For information, please contact:
Manager of Special Sales
Elsevier
200 Wheeler Road, 6th Floor
Burlington, MA 01803
Tel: 781-313-4700
Fax: 781-313-4882

For information on all Focal Press publications available, contact our World Wide Web
home page at: http: //www.bh.com/focalpress

Transferred to Digital Printing 2009

Contents

Preface

Dame Judith Anderson, the Australian actress, began her career on stage. She tells this story about her first movie:

When I finished a scene, the director called me over and whispered, "Watch your eyebrows." I asked him what he meant, and he went on to explain that when you raised your eyebrows on stage it was a matter of an inch, but when you raised them in a close-up on the movie screen, it was three feet.

In that one inch to three foot equation lies a fundamental difference between stage acting and acting for television and movies. Modern stage acting has become more naturalistic and, in a way, more cinematic. Even so, in acting for film and television, there are moments, in preparation or performance, in which the actor should be aware of what the camera and microphone can do. A barely audible sigh on stage can be detected by the audience as a rising of the chest. In film, the sigh is heard and, for emphasis, can be made louder. When one knows how these things are done, this awareness, properly applied, allows the actor to develop techniques especially for the camera.

Film and Television Acting examines these techniques in detail. No matter what experience, acting method, or training, actors will be able to correlate the ideas in this book to what they already know about the craft.

All exercises in the book must be videotaped, and the close-up shot must be used as much as possible. A video cassette recorder (VCR) and monitor are necessary.

One last note. There is only one dogmatic rule in this book. When you perform the scenes: *Don't ever look at the camera!*

If you see the lens looking at you, then you have violated this rule. It is fine to be aware of where the camera is, but from that point on, it must be ignored.

You can't even sneak a peek. In close-ups, it's vital that your eyeline never shift. Many times you'll be asked to look just and inch or two on either side of the lens. It is so easy to allow your eyes to shift back toward the lens. Do not do it!

You are relating to the other actors, not to the audience. By looking into the lens you ruin the essence of the film's reality and the bond that allows the audience to suspend its disbelief.

Acknowledgments

I would like to thank the following people who consented to be interviewed especially for this book.

Norman Jewison, producer and director. Mr. Jewison's films include *In the Heat of the Night*, *The Russians Are Coming*, and *Moonstruck*.

Glenn Jordan, director. Mr. Jordan began as a theater director. He has received five Emmy Awards for television directing, including one for *Promise*, starring James Wood and James Garner. Mr. Jordan also directed *My Brother's Keeper*, starring John Lithgow.

Louise Latham, character actress. Ms. Latham has a long career in both stage and film. Her most recent stage role was in Sam Shephard's *Lie of the Mind*. One of her memorable films was Alfred Hitchcock's *Marnie*.

Jack Lemmon, actor. Mr. Lemmon has won two Academy Awards, for best performance by a supporting actor for *Mr. Roberts* and best performance by an actor for *Save the Tiger*. His most recent stage appearances were in *Tribune* and *The Iceman Cometh*. I also thank Mr. Lemmon for his gracious foreword to this book.

John Lithgow, actor. Mr. Lithgow was nominated for an Oscar for his role in *The World According to Garp* and won an Emmy for his performance in the "Amazing Stories" series. He received another Emmy for the hit series "3rd Rock from the Sun."

Don Murray, actor, producer, and director. Mr. Murray began as a stage actor. His films include *Bus Stop* with Marilyn Monroe and *The Hoodlum Priest*. His many television appearances include "Knot's Landing."

Foreword

By Jack Lemmon

There are many books on the technique of acting and rightly so. Acting is a rich, diverse art that invites analysis, experiment, and criticism. Until now there hasn't been a book that examines the particular differences between stage, film, and television. This is why I am so pleased to write the foreword for this book.

Film and Television Acting methodically examines the techniques of acting for camera and shows how they differ from stage acting. True, many of the techniques are alike, and some of the differences are minuscule. But these subtle variations can be quite obvious when blown up on the screen. Between doing too much and doing too little, there is a subtle area where things feel just right. This book gives the actor definitive techniques to find that place.

It doesn't matter what basic acting technique you use. Ian Bernard's methods are ones of modification and enhancement, rather than change. The three elements in the book—interviews, exercises, and instruction—combine to give a complete and thorough analysis of what actors should do in front of the camera. The book also takes a realistic look at the workplace and tells you what to expect on the set.

My first film was called *It Should Happen to You*, and I was fortunate enough to play the lead opposite Judy Holliday. The director was the great George Cukor, one of the finest directors for actors. In the beginning, after almost every take he would say, "Wonderful, just wonderful, but let's do it once more. Jack, give me less."

This went on for days, me acting my head off and George saying, "Less, Jack. Less."

Finally, in complete frustration, I turned to him and said, "Are you trying to tell me not to act?"

"Oh, God, yes!" he quickly replied.

When you read this book, you'll know what George Cukor meant. I believe the actor has to learn to "trust the camera." *Film and Television Acting* teaches one how to gain that trust in a logical and direct manner.

1

The Evolving Play versus the Frozen Film

Although they might deny it, actors who perform in long-running plays perform by rote at times. Rex Harrison once confessed that during the run of *My Fair Lady* there were times in the second act when he wondered what he was going to have for supper after the performance. The intrinsic nature of a stage play creates an atmosphere wherein a variety of things can happen in performance depending on the reaction of the audience. The actors often say, "it was a good audience tonight" when everything seems to click.

I have never heard a stage actor say, "It was a good performance because our rehearsal and preparation made it possible." Now you realize the rehearsal was done weeks before, so everything, theoretically, had been set. All the questions about interpretation should have been answered. Night after night they perform the same words, the same actions. But even though the actor does the same ritualistic tune-ups before each performance, each performance is different. It is this feeling that attracts so many actors to stage acting: that no matter how planned everything is, each performance is new. There is nothing like the immediate response from a live audience.

The variety of this response at any performance depends on many factors. If the actors are good enough, technically, the audience's reception always is positive even if the performances, from the actor's point of view, were just so-so.

This sense of creative discovery at each performance doesn't exist for actors in film. They must be prepared to create a part and know that as soon as it is filmed the performance will never change. Except for Woody Allen, I know of no filmmaker who, after viewing the scenes, is allowed to reshoot scenes until he or she is satisfied. The usual procedure is to shoot as many takes of the scene as needed. Then the director decides to move on. Once that decision is made, there's no turning back. To redo a scene days or weeks later is rare and is more often caused by the film's being damaged at the lab rather than a director's wishing to reshoot. This means one thing to the actor: You have one chance to get it right.

The essential thing is to determine who the character is and the choices you make in relation to this character and this particular material. You study the material pretty much the same way in stage or film, but then it is more of a technique of delivering the character in front of the camera. Laurence Olivier was talking about character work and said: "I think in the theater you can inhabit a character, but in a film, the character must inhabit you."

Louise Latham

OK, so Olivier said the character must inhabit you. But Jack Lemmon said, "I'm not as interested in how a character should behave as how he *could* behave. If I can legitimately find a way that's very exciting, then I'll push to do that." So the idea is to find the character, then perhaps go one step farther? In film and television, this is disastrous. A little bit of ham on stage becomes a feast on camera.

Most actors have no problem with going one step farther. It's called overacting. But there's a greater problem with the actor who doesn't allow that to ever happen. The fear of doing too much has led to some pretty dull performances. The trick is to find the correct, most comfortable, and honest place. One of the best ways of doing that is to listen and react, listen and react.

An actor on stage has two reactive elements to deal with—the other actors and the audience. Because each actor senses audience reactions and each in his or her own way behaves differently because of that, we have an everchanging play from moment to moment. A film actor has no such feedback. When the scene is over, the director may offer suggestions to modify the performance, but while the scene is being filmed, you are on your own.

The expression goes: The director asked for a close-up and there was nobody home. It means the eyes were vacant, not a thought could be seen.

How do you keep somebody home?

2
Listening and Reacting

I can't prove it, but I would surmise that every child in the world at one time complained, "Nobody ever listens to me." Experts are hired by large corporations to give seminars on how to listen. It is quite probable there would be no more war if people listened to one another. Listening is the vital first link in communication. Because acting is an artistic form of communication, one would think that actors were superb listeners. They're not.

The Reaction Shot

We all know you can do a lot without saying anything in behavior. . . . You can do more with one eyebrow sometimes than ten lines of dialogue. If you can do it with a look, it might be better.

Robert De Niro

In the movies and television there is something called the *reaction shot*. This is a close shot in which one actor is listening to another actor and reacts to what is being said. (There is no such animal in the theater.) The reaction shot is often used to reinforce how the director wants the audience to respond. The actor listens and reacts. The audience empathizes and does likewise.

The reaction shot in the process of editing is used to cover up a technical glitch or a bad performance from the other actor. It is also used in editing for dramatic pause and comic timing. The pace of a movie depends on this editing process when the editor has a choice of different shots. For example, Actors One and Two are in a shot that encompasses both of them. (This is the master shot.) The scene is repeated with only Actor One, then again with

Actor Two alone in the shot. There are now three versions of the scene. With their choice of which shots to use, you can see how the director and editor can control the timing. You can also see how they can cut away from the speaking actor to the listening actor, controlling dramatic emphasis as well.

The reaction shot is one of the most important elements of film acting. It is usually done in close-up or over the other actor's shoulder immediately after the master has been shot. You as the reacting actor may or may not have lines to speak. The important thing is to hear the words spoken and make the audience believe you have never heard them before.

One may often hear a director say, "Keep alive!" Loosely translated this means, "Think! Keep thinking!" In preparing a stage role, actors do their homework by making character biographies, plotting and analyzing scenes, and doing whatever it takes to play the part. They react according to the material and to the other characters. Film and television actors usually perform the same process, but they must take it a step farther.

One never knows when those close-ups will occur. That means the actor, at any time, can be called on for a reaction shot. Let's say, for instance, the actor who is speaking is going on about a school he went to back in Ohio. The speech is four lines long. In addition to other factors, the reacting actor loves the character who is speaking. The speech is ten seconds long. This is a very long time on the screen. Does the reacting actor play ten seconds of love?

That one emotion may be enough, but then it may not. Because you don't know before shooting when these reaction shots may happen, you must prepare in a general way. Then the subtleties of film acting come into play.

A stage actor may prepare a subtext with one idea, one objective, and that usually suffices. A film actor has the opportunity to take this moment and play a variety of emotions. (Of course, they must be appropriate to the scene.) It is possible for the editor to use this one close-up in other scenes if needed. In other words, if the actor has a variety of emotions, the shot can be used in a variety of places. Editors sometimes steal a shot from one scene and put it some place else in the movie. (That is, providing locale and costume are the same.) One must be careful that the variety of emotions is not overdone. Time and time again the actor must remember that what seems normal for the stage will appear too much for the camera. It's best to keep the thought process in a related channel, that is, love, first kiss, special place, the thought of marriage, children, honeymoon, and so on.

The reaction shot, to be effective, depends entirely on the ability of the actor to listen.

Listening

It's fatal to act in film. Listening is the most important thing.
Think about what is being said.

Rex Harrison

The actor on stage stands with head cocked to one side. The face is intent. The body is tense. All of the signs point to an actor listening to another actor. The audience believes it. The director at the back of the house believes it. Even the other actor in the scene believes it. Yet it is possible for the listening actor to fool everyone at that moment. Like Rex Harrison, when he wondered about supper, the actor can wander off and lose focus (it doesn't matter what you call it) and not be able to get back. At one time or another, every actor has done it. Expressions such as *going up, drawing a blank,* and *losing one's place* all stem from this lapse of focus.

Most of the time, the actor clicks in, and no one except the actor is the wiser. Going up begins with the actor's conscious knowledge of the other actor's lines. They become not words but cues. They've been heard in rehearsal and at each performance. The words lose their meaning, and the actors no longer listen to them. They pretend to. Pretending to listen can work on stage but never in film or television.

Listening doesn't merely mean you're supposed to look at someone and listen to the words. It is listening to the real intent behind what the hell they're doing. No man did that better than Spencer Tracy. He could hold you for five minutes while somebody else was talking. . . . He may be looking around, looking at the floor, but you could tell something was going on in his mind. The problem for an actor is to reach the point where he trusts himself to just think. I still, and always will, find it difficult at times to trust myself. It is seldom that I think I've been guilty of underacting. When I'm wrong, or off, it will usually be because I've done too much.

Jack Lemmon

There is a story about Marlon Brando when he made a picture called *The Freshman.* Mr. Brando purposely didn't learn his lines. Instead, he had a small speaker put in his ear so that when it was his time to speak, a person told him his line via the speaker, then Brando delivered the line. The reason for this, the story goes, is that Brando wanted to be sure that each line was fresh, and the time he spent listening to his line before speaking it would assure that the timing was correct. Because most actors, no, make that *all* actors, will never have this kind of treatment, it is necessary to discover a technique to achieve the same results.

Spencer Tracy was reported to have said, "Know your lines, show up on time, and don't bump into the furniture." Mr. Tracy had the ability to know his lines in such a way that the audience had the impression he had just thought of them a moment before speaking. I've heard a few actors say they purposely don't memorize the lines to keep them fresh. I think this is an excuse for laziness and poor technique. Because of that, they end up paraphrasing, which is discussed later.

Knowing your lines gives you the freedom to listen and react in an honest, emotional way.

EXERCISE 1: LISTENING

The camera is in close-up on the listening actor. The questioning actor (off camera but very close to it) waits for an answer, then goes to the next question. The two actors should have eye contact, and at no time should the actor on camera look into the lens.

The following are sample questions, but you may substitute questions of your own. In fact, it is better to have fresh questions for each actor if the exercise is done in a group.

Questions

1. How old are you?
2. Where is Mount Everest?
3. Where were you two years ago?
4. What is your favorite movie?
5. Are you in love?
6. Does the camera bother you?
7. Why do you wish to be an actor?
8. What do you like most about me?

The idea is to mix unemotional, easy questions with ones that might have more emotional content. Play back the tape without sound and see if you can pick out the questions according to the reaction of the actor. (See Exercise 2 before showing playback.) Then play the tape with sound, closing your eyes. Be aware of the time between the questions and the answers. If it is a factual question with a genuine effort to answer, study the thinking process. The same goes for an emotional question. After this, play the tape in a normal manner looking at the entire performance (see Exercise 2).

A more advanced version has the off-camera questioner ask follow-up questions on the same subject. For example:

Q: Where is Mount Everest?
A: I don't know.
Q: Is it in Canada?
A: I don't think so.
Q: Could you take a guess as to where it is?
A: I really don't know.
Q: Think!

The questioner becomes an interrogator, adding another element to the game.

One would hope that reacting is the direct result of listening. Unfortunately, this isn't true. Even in exercises such as the foregoing, a clever actor plays the game intellectually and remains uninvolved emotionally. The fact is that listening is safe; reacting is not. You can listen technically, but reacting demands involvement.

When actors see themselves for the first time on playback there are many reactions. Most are self-conscious. Nervous giggles. Embarrassed denials. Some can't take it and close their eyes. The reactions, even though modified by the presence of the group, are honest.

EXERCISE 2: VIDEOTAPED REACTIONS

Videotape the actors watching themselves on the video from Exercise 1. Then play back the new tape.

Note that the actors watch their images with a critical eye that has nothing to do with artistic judgment. They see their physical faults, their hopes, and their ambitions. They see how others might see them, and most important, they see a history of themselves right up to the very moment they have just experienced.

The reaction is not to mere words but to a myriad of complex ideas and emotions. An actor in character must be able to listen and react in a similar manner. Because of the camera and its ability to detect the lie, the actor has to learn to overcome the fear of being known and vulnerable.

If the character inhabits you but part of you has been withdrawn, you are cheating the character.

When an actor has a phone conversation in one of my pictures, I always put the other actor off camera doing their part of the conversation. It isn't that I don't trust the on-camera actor to be able to act out the conversation with the appropriate pauses, etc. It's just that somehow it isn't real unless they are actually having a phone conversation.

Norman Jewison

EXERCISE 3: THE PHONE CALL

Actors One and Two sit side by side and both look into camera. The lines must be memorized word for word. Before performing the exercise, both actors decide on the subtext they will use in the scene. But each actor keeps this information secret until he or she has done the scene and the playback session is over.

> ONE
>
> Hi.

> TWO
>
> Hi.

> ONE
>
> I'm calling to say good-bye.

> TWO
>
> Oh?

> ONE
>
> It's just uh . . . well uh . . .

> TWO
>
> Look, I'm in the middle of something. May I call you back?

> ONE
>
> Oh . . . I'm sorry. If it's more important, just forget about it.

> TWO
>
> Wait! It's OK. . . . Go on . . . you were saying?

> ONE
>
> I said, if you're busy I'll call back.

                    TWO
I just said it's OK.

                    ONE
It isn't OK. It never is OK. I'm calling
to say something important and
you're telling me you're in the middle
of something. You're always in the
middle of something!

                    TWO
Just hold it. Let's just calm down.
There's no need to get worked up.

                    ONE
I'm calm ... I'm very calm.

                    TWO
Good ... I'm listening.

There is a long pause in which ONE hangs up the phone.

                    TWO
So ... you're going on a
trip? ... Hello? ... Hello? ...

TWO hangs up.

                              END OF SCENE
_____

Before playback, the actors reveal their subtexts. After playback and discussion of whether they succeeded, the scene is played again, this time with an agreed objective from both actors. That is, they share the knowledge of who they are and what their relationship is. The actors then examine the difference between that version and the one in which the objectives were known.

The latter should have moments of emotional history in which the unspoken words take on more significance. The reactions then emanate from a personal knowledge of the other's character. In other words, make the subtext, not the words, the important element.

Write similar scenes using this technique and again see if you can tell the difference between shared objectives and separate ones.

There is a caution to doing scenes written especially for exercise purposes. One tends to become lazy or a so-called soap-opera actor. I think the reason for this is the scene's lack of pedigree. There is no play, no plot, no famous author to authenticate the words; one only has the words themselves. The actor, trying to give the role importance and meaning, might overemphasize the drama and make it into melodrama. The only thing to do is to be aware of the danger and try to take steps to overcome it. This is not to denigrate actors in soap operas in any way. There are many fine actors in that field. My purpose is to point out a kind of naturalism that has become a soap-opera style of acting.

When you watch a soap opera, you'll notice that scenes often end with a close-up of a character immediately after a confrontation with another character. The camera stays on the shot for a long time. The actor is required to react specifically to what has just happened. The last line heard is usually provocative enough to help the actor. After a second or two, however, the actor resorts to pretending to think. Like pretending to listen, pretending to think may work on stage, but never on camera. This condition can easily be recognized when the actor consciously makes facial moves—lips pursing, eyes moving, tongue in cheek. It becomes technical. The motivation is no longer the text but the time needed for the music to swell and the picture to fade. The next time you watch a soap, look for this shot. Compare it with the reaction shots in the movies named at the end of the chapter.

EXERCISE 4: PHONE CALL 2

The actor on camera is in close-up and listens. The speaking actor is (1) mother, (2) lover, (3) someone the listener doesn't really like. The actor speaks the lines exactly the same way each time. Do the three characters in order on the same take.

> SPEAKING ACTOR
> Well, I'm glad you finally answered.
> We were all kind of worried. I've
> been thinking about what you said.
> Maybe you're right. Maybe things did
> get a little out of hand. But I don't
> think that I'm entirely to blame. I
> know I said some things. . . . I was
> just angry. Anyway, you left so
> abruptly, I didn't have a chance to
> say anything. We'll get together and
> talk about it. You'll see. Everything
> will be OK.

> END OF SCENE

Look for the subtle differences depending on who speaks. Perhaps for the mother and lover, the listening actor may find a place to change direction, that is, making a new choice. The main thing is to not play only one emotion. You may substitute another type of character for the speaker.

The criterion, once again, is honesty. Do you believe it? Is the actor, as the character, truly listening and then reacting? Most important: Does the camera, in close-up, reveal character every single moment?

Films to Study

Watch the following videotapes with particular regard for listening and reacting.

City Lights. Directed by Charles Chaplin. This is a silent picture with a broad style, but there are scenes at the end in which Chaplin, without words, truly shows what the thinking actor can do. An example is the scene in which the flower girl realizes that the tramp is the one who is her benefactor.

Reversal of Fortune. Directed by Barbet Schroeder. Jeremy Irons, as the passive observer in his own drama, gives a taciturn character a variety of emotions.

Sophie's Choice. Directed by Alan J. Pakula. Meryl Streep, one of the great technicians of all time, is also a wonderful actress. Note the variety of choices she makes throughout the film, especially when she listens.

Inherit the Wind. Directed by Stanley Kramer. Spencer Tracy is a master at listening.

3

Blocking and Business

Definition

I'll begin by defining what I mean by blocking and business. *Blocking* is determining where you physically move during the scene. It is the choreography of acting. *Business* is what you do in the confines of the blocking. For example, an actor walks to the desk, picks up the telephone book, and rifles through it. After a pause she puts down the phone book and takes up a picture frame.

The blocking is the walk to the desk. The business is the picking up of the phone book and the picture frame. Simply put, blocking is where you go, and business is what you do when you get there. When you apply this to the real world, it translates to this: The director can tell you were to go, but it's usually up to you to do something when you get there.

Technical Blocking

Performance for stage gives an actor much more freedom than film performance. Although it is true that certain bits of business in plays are done on specific lines, there is room for variation each time an actor performs. A stage actor can walk to within three feet of a door or, if he chooses, can make it two feet. The one-foot difference will not be noticed or, for that matter, ever be mentioned.

A film actor, however, cannot take that kind of license. That one-foot discrepancy almost always makes the director yell, "Cut!" The reason is purely technical. It has nothing to do with how well or badly one acted. The fact is that cameras do not see as human beings do. The lens of a camera can only keep so much detail in focus. During rehearsal, the camera operator measures the distances from the lens to the actor. These distances are marked down, and the camera assistant moves the lens to accommodate the focus. So if you move to three feet from the door at rehearsal and move to two feet from the door during the take, chances are you will be out of focus because of the limitations of the lens.

When shooting a film, the actors mark a scene for the camera crew just so the crew can get these measurements. Marking a scene means the actor goes through the motions, simply saying the lines without emotion so the technical problems can be solved. On big budget pictures, the stars usually have their stand-ins do most of this work. (A stand-in is a person who marks the scene for the actor.) When it comes closer to the time to do the scene, the star also participates in this technical rehearsal and for good reason. Besides the camera operator, the sound technician and boom operator need a rehearsal so they can conduct a volume check and make sure their microphones can pick up the dialogue and are out of camera range.

Good actors use this time to do their homework. They can measure the number of steps it takes to get to the door. They can make a note always to turn the same way at each rehearsal. Most important, they can assure the technical personnel that there will be no surprises when it comes time to shoot.

Technical mistakes can rob an actor of precious energy. To go through a take, getting the emotions right where you want them, only to hear "Cut" because you wandered out of camera range is not only frustrating but also very expensive. It is no accident they call it the movie *business.* Time is money, and on a movie set, it's big money.

Scenes in film and television are usually shot first as masters. A master shot is one in which most of the action in the scene can be seen by the camera. The actors get to do the scene from beginning to end, and the actors establish the moves and actions they must repeat when the coverage is shot.

Coverage is the sum total of all shots of the same scene that isolate certain elements. For example, the master scene is between two people sitting on a sofa. One gets up and goes to the door, pauses there for a line, then leaves. The coverage of this can include the following shots:

1. A medium shot of Actor One on the sofa from Actor Two's point of view.
2. A similar medium shot of Actor Two from Actor One's point of view.
3. A close-up of Actor One.
4. A close-up of Actor Two.
5. A pan or moving shot as Actor One goes to the door and turns.
6. A reversal of the previous shot to show Actor Two still sitting on the couch.
7. A shot of Actor One leaving.

This can be a two-minute scene, but you can see that without any retakes, the actor performs the same scene, or portions of it, seven times. Some of you will say, "Part of the time the camera isn't even on me." This is true. But it doesn't mean you can let down on your performance. Imagine yourself as an on-camera actor with your partner not giving any emotion to the scene. The fact is, you're always on, whether or not the camera is pointing at you. Dirk Bogarde was said to get into costume and makeup just to help his fellow actor do reaction shots.

The technical details of blocking must become automatic so you can attack the performance with a clear mind. The movements also must be done with a sense of spontaneity. Many times I have heard the complaint that this regimented behavior is the death of creativity. Their philosophy would have you believe that all creation is haphazard, wanton, and capricious. They claim that Stravinsky didn't bother to learn counterpoint, Picasso couldn't draw the figure, and actors are born, not made. The fact is just the opposite. What good is a film or television performance if the actor is constantly out of focus and can't be heard?

Perfecting the technical aspects of acting for film, such as hitting marks, is not the goal; it is a way to reach the goal.

One can wish to be a great hockey player, but one should learn to skate first.

Artistic Blocking Technique

All actions have a reason. Everything you do is logical, or it creates its own logic. Blocking is intrinsic to the meaning of a scene. One does not answer the phone unless one hears it ring. If you cannot, in collaboration with the director, make each action justified and reasonable, you must question the movement or action.

An old theatrical joke goes like this:

Actor: What's my motivation?
Director: You'll do it because I told you to.

So you get a piece of business, and you can't find a reason to justify it. The director listens to your arguments and says, "Just do it!"

You can quit. You can do it automatically. Or you can invent a reason and use it to get by. It may be a stretch or feel strange to you, but it's up to you to make it work. This is a rare event, but I can assure you it will happen at some point. Norman Jewison said that when he encounters an actor who has trouble with the blocking or handling a prop, he tries to change it to make the actor comfortable. But he adds that sometimes it isn't possible to make the change. You must prepare for those moments.

Good directors know what the camera sees, and they block for that. They also block for editing. So there may be a spot in a scene that seems uncomfortable. When you mention it, the director says forget it because the footage won't be used. It is just a device to get you from one place to the other to facilitate the editing. You must accept that vision. It is difficult for actors in a scene to imagine what the edited version will be like.

Stella Adler in her book *The Technique of Acting* states, "The prop is always truthful." I believe that the use of the prop should always be truthful. Unfortunately, this is often not the case.

Actors grab props and fiddle with them because they are nervous, and their hands are not attached to their brains. The rest of the body may be in character, but for some reason, hands, and to a lesser extent, arms, live a life totally removed from the character. Many actors use a very simple cure—they put their hands in their pockets. The next time you go to a community playhouse notice how often the men in particular shove their hands into their pockets. The problem is solvable, but it takes real concentration.

Situation

Two characters are best friends; one is telling the other—played by you—about something important. In the scene you invent a bit of business. You pick up a box of matches and look at the printing on it. The other actor continues to talk, and you put down the matches.

There are many ways to analyze the action. The following are two examples:

1. You have told the audience that you are distracted by the matches, which could mean that what the other actor is saying is not important.
2. The matches are an important plot point, and you have just realized the meaning. You break in excitedly and tell what you have discovered.

In both instances the audience is going to watch you pick up the matches and wonder why you did it. Your action compels the audience to watch. If you put the matches down and the scene goes on with no more reference to them, you have created a rude and bored character. Remember that you were friends at the beginning of the scene. You saw the matches and without much thought picked them up. The consequences of this action didn't occur to you. You simply believed in the old adage, "idle hands are the devil's workshop." In this case, the adage is true. Your simple action can take the audience away from the scene and thus ruin it. The speaker's words were meant to be important.

In a medium two shot, your hands are two feet high on the screen. You must also take into account that when your eyes—your focus—go away from the other actor, you are telling the audience something whether you want to or not. You are drawing its attention to yourself. *You are stealing the scene.*

If you accept the fact that the words are important, it becomes necessary for you to behave accordingly. You can't expect the audience to believe things that you contradict with your actions. That is what an actor does who, as another actor is speaking to her, looks for lint on her jacket or fiddles with her glasses. Some older stars were famous for variations on the aforementioned bits. Scene-stealing distractions were the reason W. C. Fields hated to act in scenes with dogs or children.

During your preparation you should make notes about what you want to do and where you want to do it. You should be prepared to defend your deeds with irrefutable dramatic logic. You must differentiate between blocking moves and pieces of business. Blocking moves, for the most part, are mainly the needs of the director. It is the choreography that allows creative editing choices. Pieces of business, on the other hand, are the small extras that make for extraordinary characterization.

Individuals behave in unique ways. This behavior can manifest itself overtly, adding dimension to the character. This overt behavior can be barely visible, yet influence the total performance. For example, in *Midnight Cowboy*, Dustin Hoffman decided to play the part of Ratso Rizzo with a painful-looking limp. The limp looked like the result of a childhood injury. The character was a down and out hustler who would sell his own mother for a quarter. Yet at the end of the movie I found myself in tears over his death. I believe that most audiences reacted the same way. The sight of this pathetic limp created a reservoir of good will. In spite of Ratso's despicable character, the audience forgave him his sins, and I believe they did it primarily for one reason. The painful limp contributed to what he was, and because of that, one could understand. I don't believe there has been a modern film hero quite so wretched or rotten who has evoked such sympathy. I don't think Mr. Hoffman would have achieved the same effect had he strutted through the movie on two normal legs. It was reported that Mr. Hoffman put sharp pebbles in one shoe to induce a limp. However he did it, the business paid off. The character Ratso had a limp that affected his life and in turn affected the audience.

Actors who make strong choices regarding overt behavioral characteristics had better have equally strong reasons for making them. You can almost make it a rule: *If you're going to do something big, you had better have an equally big reason for doing it!*

Jack Lemmon tells a prop story about making the film *The Apartment*. His character has a cold in a scene with a character played by Fred MacMurray.

Well, I decided to use a nasal spray. Now I'm all nervous because I think he's not going to give me a raise because he knows I've been letting executives use my apartment for hanky panky. . . . Well . . . the prop man puts milk in the nasal spray because the picture's in black and

*white, and when the spray shoots out you'll really see it. I didn't say
anything to Fred or to Billy Wilder, the director, and we start the scene.
In the script Fred lets me off the hook and I'm so excited I squeeze the
spray right under his nose. And all Fred did was look at it and do a slow
take, following the spray until it hit the floor and then back to me. You
hardly notice it on the screen, but for those who did, it was perfect. It
was subtle. If it was a big thing, then it would be a gag. But it happened
in the context of the scene and the characters. It was legitimate.*

Jack Lemmon

Legitimate . . . credible . . . real . . . honest . . . These words occur again and
again. They are as important to blocking and business as to any other aspect of
acting. It is extremely important to rehearse with the items you are going to
actually use. Scrutinize the set or the location. Make a mental inventory of what
is there. Chances are you'll have nothing to do with ninety-nine percent of the
stuff, but it's all usable.

EXERCISE 5: BLOCKING AND MARKS

In the following scene, the actors in rehearsal should each hit four
marks. The marks should be at least four feet away and marked with tape on the
floor. During the performance of the exercise, someone monitors the actors'
success or failure in hitting the marks by simply watching the actors' feet and
taking notes. Because a video camera has a much wider range of focus, it is
impossible to tell in the playback whether the actors are in or out of focus. But
I can assure you that with a movie camera, any missing of the marks would ruin
a take.

ONE enters, very upset. TWO watches as ONE searches for
something.

ONE
OK. Where is it?

TWO
Where is what?

ONE
That's what I truly like about you.
You always answer a question with a
question.

> TWO
> And you always say always.

> ONE
> What I always say is a direct result
> of what you always say.

> TWO
> So what you're saying is we have a
> symbiotic relationship.

ONE stops searching and comes to TWO.

> ONE
> Are you putting me on?

> TWO
> Am I putting you on what?

> ONE
> There! You did it again!

ONE walks away and searches.

> TWO
> If you'd keep better tabs on things
> you wouldn't lose them.

> ONE
> That's like saying if I knew where
> things were, they wouldn't be lost.

> TWO
> Exactly.

ONE stops and looks at TWO.

> ONE
> You know where they are don't you?

> TWO
> Yes.

> ONE
> And you let me look like a fool.

> TWO
> It breaks up the day.

> ONE
> OK, where are they?

TWO holds up the keys. ONE takes them and leaves.

END OF SCENE

The actors should repeat this scene until they can hit all the marks without being obvious. This means they must actually land on each mark, not merely close to it. The body and face must be within inches of the same position each time the actors do the scene.

The next scene is an exercise for business. Handling props naturally is a must. A film actor must be able to do repeated takes making sure that the props hit their marks each time. The routine is established at rehearsal and should never change after the first take unless the director requests something different. In the following scene, each actor decides when the business occurs and stages the scene so it can happen in a credible manner. The dialogue indicates the business.

EXERCISE 6: BUSINESS

In this exercise, the actors must be aware of which hand does what. It is also important to do the action on a given line.

Props: two glasses, a wine bottle, a corkscrew, and a telephone. Actors One and Two sit on chairs with a table in front of them. On the table are the glasses and the wine bottle. The corkscrew and phone are to their rear on another table.

The scene is to be shot as a master. The actors make notes on the action. The scene then should be covered in single medium shots of each actor.

The coverage action should match the master. For example, the bottle is held at the same height with the same hand. The glass is filled to the same level.

> ONE
> Would you like a glass of wine?

> TWO
> I don't drink.

> ONE
> One drink . . . it's good for the heart.

ONE picks up the bottle, sees that it's not opened, and searches for the corkscrew.

TWO
I'm serious, I don't drink.

ONE
You don't mind if I do then, do you?

TWO
Of course not.

ONE goes to the rear table and picks up the corkscrew. ONE
returns to the table and begins to fiddle with the bottle, having a
difficult time. TWO takes the corkscrew and the bottle.

TWO
Here, let me.

TWO deftly begins to open the bottle.

ONE
For a nondrinker, you sure know
your way with an opener.

TWO
I've had a lot of experience.

ONE
Oh, I didn't know that.

TWO
I don't advertise about it.

TWO finishes the job and hands the bottle back to ONE, who pours
a drink into the glass. ONE takes a sip and approves of the wine.

ONE
It's very good. . . . You mind if I
ask . . . uh . . . What was your
downfall?

TWO
You mean which kind of booze?

ONE
Yeah.

TWO
You name it, I drank it.

ONE
I never understood that. I know it's a
sickness and all. . . . But why can't
you just handle it?

TWO
Because we can't.

The phone rings. ONE gets up and goes to the phone. TWO picks
up the glass of wine and holds it to the light.

ONE
Hi. . . . No. . . . No. . . . Just relaxing.

ONE sees TWO looking at the wine and quickly turns away. TWO
puts the glass down, notices that ONE is not looking and quickly
picks the glass up again and starts to take a sip. Throughout this,
ONE ad-libs a quiet phone conversation. ONE casually looks to
TWO, who now has the glass near the lips. TWO catches the look
and slowly puts the glass down. ONE concludes the phone call and
comes back to the table.

ONE
You could have a sip. . . . I wouldn't
tell.

TWO
Thanks. . . . That's very nice of you.

ONE takes the glass and sips with pleasure.

ONE
You don't know what you're missing.

ONE sips again. TWO watches for a moment, then turns away.

END OF SCENE

The important thing is to create a believable scene. You should also make
note of which hand did what. Learn to handle objects the same way each time.
This way, when it comes time to edit different takes together, objects don't
mysteriously jump from one hand to the other.

Blocking and business are techniques of acting. They are not mere append-
ages that haphazardly appear at the last minute. Glenn Jordan tells of an actor

who had to pour a cup of tea while delivering some very dramatic lines. After several takes, the actor said he couldn't do the business and the lines at the same time. This is ridiculous.

The actor must control the instrument, in this case the body. Take dancing lessons, learn to fence. Practice different kinds of walks and postures. Exercise. The body language of an actor in a film provides the audience with the first clue about the character. At the onset blocking and business may be simply where the actors go and what they do. In the end, however, these things should be organic to the character. Look at the following films and pay close attention to the physical aspects of the characters—how they move and what they do. See how they handle props.

Films to Study

Mr. Hulot's Holiday. Directed by Jacques Tati. This is a modern silent film that demonstrates character through body language.

Midnight Cowboy. Directed by John Schlesinger. Both Dustin Hoffman and Jon Voight are effective.

On the Waterfront. Directed by Elia Kazan. Marlon Brando as a former prize fighter creates the character simply by walking down the street.

The Raging Bull and *Taxi Driver*. Directed by Martin Scorsese. Robert De Niro's body language in both of these films is a perfect study of character development.

4
Preparation

Stage to Film

An actor who trains for stage acting uses any number of techniques to "get into the part"—character biographies, scene analysis, sense memory exercises, and research on the play's subject matter for background material. Each of these techniques is equally appropriate for film and television preparation. At some point in the process, however, a film actor should be aware of how the performance is to be done, and this should trigger some unique ideas that apply only to camera techniques.

In the modern theater you get a lot of deals between the audience and the actor: I'll pretend this is really happening if you pretend to believe it. And it's not a very clean deal. People are not very comfortable with that. But they've gotten used to it.

Mike Nichols

A theater audience accepts a new, tenuous reality as soon as it becomes involved with the play. The better the performance, the writing, and set design, the deeper is the acceptance.

I believe the "deals" Mr. Nichols is talking about have more to do with the limitations of the theater genre itself. Whereas a stage play often may refer to big events that occur off stage, a film must show them. Whereas a stage actor is allowed a poetic voice whose words paint the picture, a film actor is actually *in* the picture, and telling is superfluous. The stage setting may consist of fragments and symbols. It is the rare film that does not emulate reality.

The deal is, this isn't real and we all know it. That is the magic and wonder of good theater. It is also an idea that actors must forget when they venture into film and television.

One often hears, "I'm an actor, I can play anything." More often than not, when it applies to theater, this is quite true. If the actor creates an illusion skillfully, the audience accepts it. In the theater, men play women, women play men, men and women play animals, and so forth. This theatrical license is an essential part of many play productions. But even the most naturalistic play still has elements of being theatrical. In no sense do I mean *theatrical* to conjure ideas of overblown amateurish acting, exaggerated gestures, and florid speech.

Let me define what I mean by the word *theatrical*. After the play is written, rehearsed, rewritten, and fine-tuned, the next logical step is the performance. All the aforementioned elements are redefined each time the play is performed. This transformation begins with the actors preparing in their dressing rooms and the audience taking its seats. It is completed when the actors take their bows and the audience leaves.

This is a theatrical event. I contend that the actor's knowledge of this event during rehearsal has a subconscious effect on preparation. All the techniques used in rehearsal are influenced by this knowledge. For example, knowing the size of the theater and the stage has a direct relation to voice projection and stage blocking.

Actors in a play, when they get up in the morning, know that at eight o'clock that night, they will perform. Their whole day is geared to that fact. Actors in film have no idea when they will be called upon to do a scene. After the call, it could be ten minutes or it could be five hours. Then, an assistant comes and there you are in front of the camera and you have to do it!

Glenn Jordan

An actor preparing for film or television also should have a vision of what the "event" will be. The event in this case is the time the performance is shot on film or tape.

In film, unlike the theater, you're looking for the physical look, the age, the type, even the color of the eyes or the hair. Now you can play parts on stage way past your age. But in film, to accomplish that, we have to go through a tremendous make-up process, prosthetics, etc., all of which is time consuming and expensive. In other words, casting in a film becomes more intense, more pragmatic.

Norman Jewison

What has this to do with preparation? Everything. *It is essential that actors know who they are and what they look like. They must define themselves before preparation.*

You Are You

It sounds a little superficial, doesn't it, like one of those self help books. After all, they're not buying you, they're buying your talent. But maybe the real you is nothing like the perceived you. Maybe you think and act tall; you look in the mirror and see a sensitive face and a sweet disposition, yet you're looked upon by some as short, brutish, and sullen.

Will your best friends tell you the awful truth?

The idea of what a leading man or leading woman should look like changes from year to year. So I'm not talking about handsome, good looking, pretty, beautiful, or any other fashionable quality. But, to be realistic, most actors who become movie stars do have generally appealing physical looks, looks generated by audience tastes.

Knowing who you are and what you look like saves a great deal of wasted effort in trying to cram yourself into parts that simply won't work. Prepare for what you believe will be the most likely casting for you. Don't practice the violin if you're to give a piano recital. In *No Acting Please* Eric Morris and Joan Hotchkis write: "I came to realize that while there's lip service paid to using your personal life on stage and getting 'deep' into your own emotions, few actors have the courage to do this, and most teachers aren't even aware of the necessity for this kind of search."

The following exercise is not meant to reveal your innermost secrets, nor does it necessitate an intrusion into your privacy. The personal questions have to do with your public self: your self perception. It is your choice as to how far you wish to go in answering.

EXERCISE 7: WHO AM I?

Prepare the following list, then recite it on camera:

1. Your body measurements: feet, legs, torso, arms, hips, waist, head, height.
2. Describe eyes, teeth, hair, complexion, smile.
3. Describe interests, likes and dislikes, hobbies, goals.
4. Describe what's best and what's worst about yourself and what you would most like to change.
5. Describe where you wish to be ten years from now.
6. Describe what you are doing to attain your goals.

After playback, first ask yourself whether you stand by the answers. Then the group frankly and gently tells with which points they agree and disagree.

This undoubtedly leads to a few bad jokes, but remember that all members of the group must participate, so whoever gives is in line to receive.

The necessity of complete honesty in this exercise correlates with one fact in the film and television world: because of the way film and television are cast, you will, more often than not, be playing characters that resemble you both physically and emotionally. When the audience first sees you on the screen, its first impression should eliminate pages of exposition.

Laurence Olivier said the character inhabits you, and I believe it is your persona that is cast in film and television. It is you and the vision of you in the part that stimulates the director to want to see more. *Typecasting* may be the pejorative word to describe it. But that concept defines an era in which casting-couch stories were likely to be true. Modern filmmakers, although not immune to such activities, have such a variety of opinions regarding type that actors of all sizes, shapes, and ages are cast into all kinds of parts. Now more than ever talent and ability seem to be the criteria.

Most actors begin their careers by doing bit parts of a couple of lines and screen time of two minutes or even less. The actor is usually handed only the pages that encompass the part. (A Screen Actors Guild rule intended to prevent this practice is often ignored.) Through begging or knowing someone or with simple luck, you may be able to get your hands on the entire script. But don't count on it. The problem is to know how you fit into the mosaic. Don't ever believe that a measly two lines can't get you noticed. It has before, and it will again. Careers have been launched with less.

You'll undoubtedly read for the part and generally know who the character is. When you're cast, the first thing to do is research the job or situation your character is involved in.

> *Pudovkin, the Russian director, believed if you wanted a actor to play a policeman, why don't you hire a policeman! Because he will behave and do exactly what he does everyday and he will be more believable than an actor trying to play a policeman. That works fine until it comes time for the real policeman to say lines. . . . So, in a film, the director is often looking for someone that maybe doesn't have the experience of a well-known actor, but he will overlook that if he can get someone who is perfect for the part in his mind's eye.*
>
> Norman Jewison

Let's say you're cast as a detective. All of us have seen detectives in film and television time and time again. And each of us has a clichéd idea of how they should behave. To avoid these clichés, one should first examine what detectives do, not who they are.

You have to know how to talk to actors. Directors who don't, talk to them about feeling, but directors who do, will talk to them about doing. You don't ever say to an actor, "Get mad at this guy." What you might say is, "You let that person know, if he tries this again, you're going to murder him. And make damn sure that you see in his eyes and he understands how serious you are." Because that's a doable thing. You can take a nonactor, and if you can get them to relax emotionally and think a thought, you'll see it with the camera. You couldn't do that onstage.

Sydney Pollack

The key phrase is *doable thing*. Meyerhold, a great Russian stage director, once said: "Words were the decoration on the skirts of action." You must know what your character—in this case, a detective—does. It is also essential to know that besides being a detective, the person is a human being. Too often, an actor picks up the aura of a profession and the audience sees a one-dimensional performance.

As soon as you read *detective*, most of you thought of film and television detectives, not the real thing. Most of us have seen a large number of movies, and we are prejudiced because of it. We've seen every profession portrayed, rich people, poor people, cowboys, senators. You may not consciously remember the actor in the part, but chances are, the impression of the role has made its mark. In the detective category, the private eye has become a genre. But let's say you're not playing Sam Spade or Phillip Marlowe—what do you do?

Your concept of *detective* should begin with what a detective does then proceed to what unique characteristics you can add to the part.

One caution: be wary of simulating nothing but the truth. We'll stick with a detective as an example. Most of the work is plain dull. It entails endless paperwork, boring interviews, and long hours when nothing happens. You can be sure the script will not reflect that kind of person. Yet as a good actor, you are trying to be real, honest. Even with chases, car crashes, and bodies being discovered every five minutes, it is possible.

The trick is to let the script speak for itself. Put your character into that world. Don't try to enhance it. Just live in it. With your solid preparation, your character exists truthfully, no matter how unreal some of the situations may be. A good example is a recent television show called "Cop Rock," which was a noble failure. "Cop Rock" had some fine acting and a lot of acting situations that were unusual. For instance, many times the drama stopped while the actors went into a wild rock-and-roll musical number, complete with choreography. After the song finished, the actors went right back into the drama. The scenes were as real as you can get. The musical numbers were played as script continuations, but nevertheless they were musical numbers. The actors never lost focus. They reacted truthfully to situations, no matter how unusual.

More often though, the actor is cast into a weekly program that has established dramatic parameters that, to be generous, are not exactly Shakespearean. (Some scholars believe that Shakespeare was not exactly Shakespearean.) Remember, you can't change the destiny of the program by offering literary suggestions to make it better. By making your part better, you'll accomplish all that you can.

The bromide goes, "There are no small parts, there are only small actors." If you make the most of what you have without going overboard, you're doing the job.

Preparation for featured or starring roles is somewhat more complex. Now you have the entire script and you know the story. What do you do?

> *I read the script over and over again. First I try to understand what the script means, and once I think I understand what it means overall, then I read it once more concentrating on my character's lines. I read it aloud, not trying to give the lines any expression, just to familiarize myself with the words. I want the words to be familiar in my head so when I finally do them in performance they come easily and naturally. Then I come to the first day of rehearsal. I put my script in front of me, no matter how familiar I am with it. When another character speaks to me, first I will listen, then I will let whatever reaction that creates happen. I won't force this reaction. After this I'll check my reply in the script, look at the other actor, and say my line. From the beginning, I will start contact with the other actor and let my performance come out of a combination of the emotions they stir in me, the text itself, and the guidance the director offers.*
>
> *Don Murray*

Out of Order

One of the most difficult acting problems in film and television is the simple fact that scripts are shot out of order. Page 30 on Monday . . . Page 12 on Tuesday. On page 30, you're locked in a mental ward for the criminally insane. Page 12, you're a happily married churchgoer. That means you're at the dramatic peak the day before you shoot the build-up.

I'm exaggerating the plot circumstances a bit. Most scripts don't have such a drastic change. But that makes acting even more difficult. The more subtle the change, the more difficult it is to solve the acting problem. It is essential to plot an emotional strategy throughout a script. Because you do many scenes back and forth in time, you must know where the character is at any given moment.

The director approaches a scene with the whole film in mind. It is our job to see how this scene fits into the mosaic. The director is the only person who knows what the effect of the whole film will have on an audience. At least, theoretically we hope that's so. The actor is saying, "Wait a minute, I wouldn't do that. Why would I do that!" That's when I have to say, "You do that because don't you remember on page four that such and such happened! And we haven't shot that yet. Let's go back and read the pages that affect this scene." You should constantly go back and do your homework while they're setting up so you know where you're going to be emotionally.... Sometimes actors don't do that. They play each scene separately. That's why directors and actors have to have a very close relationship. A little bit closer than it is in the theater.

Norman Jewison

Before continuing, it may be best to explain why film and television movies are not usually shot in the order they're written—TIME AND MONEY. If the crew is on a set, ready to shoot, it is most efficient to shoot all subsequent scenes that take place on the same set. All scenes that take place in, let's say, the living room, will be shot while the crew is in that locale. This makes it necessary for all members of the crew to take notes on all sorts of technical details that pertain to where each scene occurs in the story. For example, they must document the time of year, the hairstyles of the actors, the set design, and the wardrobe. Like these tangible things, the actors' comprehension of story and character must fit into a logical time line. Audiences are not aware of this hodgepodge when they watch the film. And that's the way it must be.

How do you become the character?

You know how you grow mushrooms! You put them in a cold, damp place, and you feed them shit. That's basically what acting is. You put out the best set of circumstances that would make it possible for this thing (character) to grow, and then you trust. You really have to be accessible.

Debra Winger

Don't take the word *accessible* to mean that you are a hollow shell waiting for the director to fill in the parts. No directors want puppets. Glenn Jordan states that he always wants the actor to come in with a choice, even if it's wrong. Directors welcome your ideas as long as you have not cast them in cement.

> *There are some actors who bring in their performance as some sort of a gift that's already wrapped. They prepare in a way that has nothing to do with the director or the other actors. It can be done very skillfully. And sometimes in film, because of time constraints, some actors do it that way.*
>
> *Don Murray*

Mr. Murray has a point. You get the part Thursday night for a Friday morning start. You'll meet the other actors in make-up, and, if you're lucky, you'll get a chance to run lines. On the set, you have a couple of walk-throughs to set the blocking, and then the director calls for a take. What happens now really depends on what happened last night.

Using the script as a blueprint, the actor first notes all major plot changes—story points at which something happens that sends the script off in another direction. Then within those major changes, the actor can make a subtext, noting the emotional and textual reasons behind the character's behavior. Actors should be aware of possibilities to make subtle differences in regard to how they react to different characters. Is this the kind of person who is brusque to waitresses and obsequious to policemen?

The notes need not be extensive. In fact, one-word clues can be sufficient. The problem with going on and on writing essays on character is this: the brain takes over. An intellectual analysis is fine as long as you remember that characters, even very smart characters, behave the way they do because of feelings. Some may repress the feelings magnificently, but they're still there.

Another thing to note: Ask yourself the question why the other characters behave the way they do toward you. Mike Nichols in an interview stated: "When I teach acting, I tell my students that it's important not to make up your mind about your character, not to present the audience with a conclusion, because something closed is not as interesting or alive as something open. And people are endlessly surprising. Surely the greatest thing in a character, whether in a book or a play or a movie, is just that: the sense of surprise."

I'm quite sure that Mr. Nichols means for the actor to prepare but to leave space for things to happen. As Don Murray said: "Don't bring the gift in all neatly packaged." Lazy actors bring neither the gift nor the preparation. Their rationale is that talent will see them through. They assure the director that it will "be there" when the camera rolls. Too many times this is allowed to happen because the director casts the actor on the basis of a past performance and feels a wary trust. My feeling is that there are a lot of talented actors in this world, and most directors prefer the ones who come prepared.

Re: When lines should be known in rehearsal.

The freedom of improvisation was last week, and you can't get that freedom back unless you have mastery of the material. The spur of the moment has to come of actually knowing what is and what isn't.

Peter Brook

Sidney Lumet is a strong believer in rehearsal. He feels that if you rehearse correctly, you don't lose spontaneity. Rehearsal gives actors the entire arc of the role, which gives them the freedom to find that magical accident.

On the other hand, Woody Allen never gives any actor the entire script. Even the leads in his movies get only their parts. What is more, no one gets any explanation of what went on before or will go on later. Allen expects the actor to play the scene. This may or may not involve a certain amount of improvisation, but the main fact is, actors get to see the whole movie only when it plays in a theater.

This brings up an important issue about auditioning, which is discussed later. When you are handed the script (the sides), it is the director's choice to give you a detailed explanation or not. If not, it is up to you to analyze the scene as best you can and to play it.

A word about preparation: In the context of the script, know the locale, the time of the year, and why you are there. Do this, no matter how small the part. If it isn't explicit in the script, imagine these elements. Finally, know your lines and the character's objective in each scene. And of course, listen and react.

Like a jazz musician, you should know the tune and know the chords and structure; then you may improvise. This does not mean paraphrasing the script. Paraphrasing is a bad habit borne of poor technique and sometimes an inflated ego. Actors who don't bother to learn the lines as written usually make the excuse that the script is poorly written. Once the habit of paraphrasing is begun, it is difficult to stop. The situation may arise in which the director wrote the script or the writer is present, and there you are for the first time, compelled to say the lines as written. If you have trouble with a line, try to find a way to make it work. But if the problem won't go away, discuss it with the director. Don't improvise unless the director suggests it.

Some actors take short cuts in preparation and succeed. To my mind, this is a hit-or-miss approach that can backfire seriously. You may have one

lliant performance and wait years for another. I agree with Sidney
umet. Strong preparation is more apt to allow that magical accident to
happen.

EXERCISE 8: STAGE VERSUS FILM PERFORMANCE

One set of actors prepares the following scene as a stage performance.
Blocking is for the stage. Another group prepares for a film or television performance. Videotape the stage performance with a long shot using a stationary
camera. The film performance should be shot much closer; move the camera if
you wish.

ONE
If I said that I was very, very ill,
what would you think?

TWO
I'd think you had AIDS.

ONE
Right. . . . And what else would you
think?

TWO
I'd think you were gay.

ONE
Then what else?

TWO
And you hadn't said anything to me.

ONE
Betrayed, huh?

TWO
Nothing that drastic.

ONE
You're prejudiced.

TWO
I am not.

ONE
You have a clichéd, prejudicial mind.

TWO
Why? Because I associated AIDS with gays?

ONE
Exactly. What if you're wrong about me?

TWO
What if! What if you get the hell out of here. Go play your games with someone else.

ONE
No one else has such an interest. Is that clear, or do I have to spell it out?

TWO
You've given it to me.

ONE
That's funny.

TWO
You bastard! My God . . . Oh my God! How could you do that?

ONE
I know you'll deny it, but I want you to know that I know what you did. I just wanted to see whether or not you'd try to put the blame on me.

TWO
You're OK?

ONE
No thanks to you. I've waited a long time for you to say something.

One starts out.

ONE
I hope it was worth it.

> TWO
> Matter of fact it was.

> ONE
> I guess we'll just have to wait to find
> out. See you.

> TWO
> We used protection.

> ONE
> Did you?

> TWO
> . . . No . . . look at the odds.

> ONE
> I don't have to. You're the one who's
> taken the gamble.

ONE leaves. TWO reacts.

END OF SCENE

I've chosen a "hot" dramatic subject so the actors can better differentiate the two versions. Try to ignore the filming techniques and concentrate on the acting. Note the difference from line to line. Even if the characters in each version have no correlation, look for the technique in each. Do the gestures, the relationships, the connections vary because of the film versus stage performance? Would the stage version as it was performed still seem as if it were for the theater if you used camera techniques such as close-ups? Film the stage-acting performance again, this time using close-ups, and analyze the difference between that and the film version.

Are the characters in each version equally credible?
Is the body language and business natural, meaningful?

Good technique frees the artist to create.
It also implies that the actor is always in control.

The only time I felt that I was losing it and that I was becoming the character was on Save the Tiger. *The character was having a nervous breakdown, and we were shooting in sequence. About two thirds of the way, he's starting to hallucinate, seeing dead soldiers and things like that. I suddenly found myself beginning to crack up driving to the studio. I pulled over to the side of the road, and I was sobbing. I didn't know what the hell was the matter. Then I realized that the character was beginning to take over. I said, "My God." From that moment on, it stopped. I was able to separate them. It was a rare situation, and it hasn't happened since. You have to be into it very deeply but still have the ability to watch and analyze yourself.*

Jack Lemmon

Today's film and television industry is much more sophisticated, knowledgeable, and cautious. A well-prepared actor has a much better chance of building a career than a seat-of-the-pants talent.

One last word on preparation: Memorization of the part, running lines, and rehearsing blocking and business are certainly a part of preparation. But you must be careful that these very important ingredients don't take over. A more comprehensive description of preparation would be this: You know what the character wants every single moment and have a rationale for each action. In the abstract, you have control and can perform whatever the text demands. You have experienced similar conditions in workshops, exercises, and self study. When you are actually cast in a part, you are familiar with the problems.

Too many actors prepare only when they are cast in a part. A smart actor prepares each day for that eventuality.

5
Character

The main difference in creating character for film versus stage is this: The stage actor paints broad strokes, looking for the whole physical impression. The film actor begins with small details, looking for hidden traits. The stage actor wears the character's clothes; the film actor not only wears the clothes but also has sewn the button—the one that doesn't quite match—on the sleeve. It doesn't matter what condition the stage actor's fingernails are in, but show me the well-manicured hand of a foundry worker in a film, and I'll ask a lot of questions.

The Building Blocks

Small details accumulate, and when there are enough of them, they create a reality. In Dirk Bogarde's wonderful book, *Snakes and Ladders*, he states: "I am an actor who works from the outside in, rather than the reverse. Once I can wear the clothes which my alter-ego has chosen to wear, I then begin the process of his development from inside the layers. [Concerning wardrobe on *The Servant*], each item was carefully chosen by Losey [the director, Joseph Losey] down to the tie-pin: a tight, shiny, blue serge suit, black shoes which squeaked a little, lending a disturbing sense of secret arrival, pork-pie hat with a jay's feather, a Fair Isle sweater, shrunken, darned at the elbows, a nylon scarf with horses' heads and stirrups. A mean shabby outfit for a mean and shabby man."

In film, it is more likely that if the script says *antique vase*, it will be just that. Many films today are shot on location, so the streets, the buildings, the rooms function in real life as they do in the film. It is the actor's job to fit into these environments as if he or she belonged there.

Quoting again from *Snakes and Ladders*, "With Losey, one also discovered the value of textures. The textures of things; of wood, of metal, of glass, of the petals of a flower, the paper of a simple playing card, of snow even, and fabric. Plaster wood, however well combed, does not feel like wood, neither does it photograph like wood; nylon is not silk, fiber glass is not steel, a canvas door does not close with the satisfying sound or weight of mahogany.

All these apparently trivial items, or obvious if you like, add up to an enormous whole. And the actor feels the reality. It is, of course totally cinematic, not theatrical. In the theater almost nothing must be real. It is reality extended."

Lord Laurence Olivier put it this way: "I'm quite shocked to find how exaggerated stage acting is after the films. It seems to me that in the theater, audiences swallow dialogue and acting conventions which, on the screen, would draw howls of derisive laughter."

The process of building a character is complex. There is no magic formula, no method that guarantees success. But it is this very complexity that intrigues us. Like all human beings, characters have good days and bad. They behave in a consistent way, then all of sudden change direction. They are in constant flux, because stimuli change from moment to moment. Or they resist change and become rigid. Even the most passive and boring character must still be interesting enough for the audience to watch. One supposes the writer had a strong dramatic reason to write about that person, and it is the actor's job to fulfill that mission and, indeed, to enhance it.

It is a rare actor who can read a part and know from that moment on what he or she is going to do. The danger in such an act is this—the insight hits with a bang. You rehearse it and solidify it, then just as quickly as it came, you suddenly know that it is wrong. The process of undoing is more painful than doing. When you work on a character then change your mind, you may end up with a hybrid character, which in itself is fine except that you may also have lost control. You may switch from one to another choice during a performance without being aware of it.

I prefer a slow, meticulous process—making note of each detail and adding one item to another until you know who the character is. The cumulative building of character helps you to reject or accept ideas as you go along. Debra Winger stated in an *American Film* interview, "I think the biggest thing an actor can learn is trust—to trust that something is going to happen." In short, do your homework and be patient.

It would be interesting to get a part on Monday and wake up on Tuesday as the character. It is no longer your bed, your toothbrush, your clothes. Your friends and relatives are now the character's. The itches, the taste in the mouth, and the smells of the morning are no longer yours.

In this Kafkaesque dream, you have ceased to exist. The question is, Does an actor have to give up self to play a part? I don't think so. The loss of self to the character can mean that you have lost control and the ability to make intelligent decisions should circumstances in the script change. You, the real you, must learn to make intelligent decisions about the character and be able to implement them with action. The only way you can do that is to remain in control.

*You have to make choices. No director in the world can help you with
that. They can reject what they don't like, but they're yours. You're
using your craft eventually, but all the craft in the world won't help you
make choices.*

Gene Hackman

What Mr. Hackman means is that you, the person, are the ultimate choice
maker.

Intellect and Instinct

Many actors make character bios, which is fine. But first it
important to know the character's philosophy and attitude about the following
ideas.

1. Sex
2. Religion
3. Morality
4. Social customs
5. Mortality

The traits or observable manners of a character may have nothing to do
with this list. Indeed, all the real feelings may be so deeply hidden, so
expertly repressed, that we see the exact opposite of what lies beneath.
The character may show different and contradictory behavior to other
characters. One has to remember that we react to different stimuli, and even
though we appear consistent, it only takes a slight diversion to elicit a radical
change.

A person who hates the idea of romance, mocks friends in love, and dis-
avows the existence of love may turn the corner and become smitten. Actors
must always look for this proverbial corner. A test of true character is for the
actor to know the choices he or she makes under pressure. It is that moment
when the audience realizes what has been suggested all along and accepts it
because it is truthful.

*There are times when the physical aspects of the character come first.
For instance, in* Some Like It Hot, *I'm in drag for three quarters of the
picture. I was concerned with a look. The wide eyes, the curved,
lipsticked lips. I created something then crawled in and made the
character behave to suit the appearance. It was against what I've usually
done and what I've learned. But in this case I think it worked.*

Jack Lemmon

It's important to be flexible. In this case Mr. Lemmon chose a different method to create a character. It also points out that no method of acting is absolute. The variety and complexity of roles compels the actor to find the best way to be creative.

Acting is concentrated energy, living at a pitch most of us don't experience, combined with the ability to expose yourself, to tell the audience things about yourself even you don't really know, to open up and confess to ambitions or fears or fantasies normally kept hidden. It's always a mix, a balance between rigorous technical craftsmanship and wallowing in feeling.

Ian McKellen

EXERCISE 9: CHARACTER

You're a night clerk in a sleazy hotel. By day you are a student in a university. The camera is on the clerk. The voice is off camera. Write the clerk's ideas about sex, religion, morality, social customs, and mortality before performing the scene. Also write down the clerk's classes, major, and grades. Begin on the clerk's action (whatever you choose to do).

>   VOICE
> You open?

>   CLERK
> Yes.

>   VOICE
> I want a room.

>   CLERK
> That'll be six bucks.

>   VOICE
> What you looking at?

>   CLERK
> Nothing.

>   VOICE
> Is there a towel in the room?

                    CLERK
        It's a buck for towels.

                    VOICE
        For six bucks I should get a towel.

                    CLERK
        Yeah.

                    VOICE
        Look, I don't have a buck. But I want
        to shower.

                    CLERK
        It's a buck for a towel.

                    VOICE
        Gimme a break.

                    CLERK
        I can't.

                    VOICE
        One lousy towel.

                    CLERK
        I said I can't.

                    VOICE
        Why?

                    CLERK
        They check on me.

                    VOICE
    (Mocks)
        They check on me.

                    CLERK
        Use your shirt.

                    VOICE
        Thanks.

The clerk watches for a moment.

                    CLERK
        I don't make the damn rules.

VOICE
You just follow them.

CLERK
If I had a dollar I'd get you a towel.

VOICE
Thanks. See you. . . .

VOICE leaves. Clerk goes back to previous action.

CLERK
What do people want from me?

END OF SCENE

The clerk's behavior should reflect some of the ideas we listed before. The scene should be prepared again. This time the student dresses the part and uses props if needed. Before retaping, write down answers to the following.

1. Favorite food
2. Self image: clothes, hair, neat, sloppy, fastidious, and so on
3. Favorite writer
4. Favorite music
5. Major peeves

Try to introduce some of these elements into the scene. Be careful you don't cram something in that obtrudes. More important is your knowledge of the character's history. I am not suggesting that any of the traits or beliefs has to become evident. They can exist only in the mind of the actor. With the ten elements in mind, tape the next scene. The setting is the same. The phone rings, and it is the clerk's mother.

EXERCISE 10: CHARACTER EXTENDED

CLERK
Hotel Rex . . . Hi . . . It's three A.M. . . .
What are you doing up? . . . Don't
be silly. I'm fine . . . I'm telling you
I'm fine. No . . . I'm studying. Got a
final on Tuesday . . . No, I'm not
taking pills . . . I know a lot of students do. I'm not . . . Yes. I drink

coffee. No, mom. I don't drink that
much. I know it's bad. . . . On Friday?
Maybe. If I'm still alive . . . I was only
joking. . . . Because this is the only job
I can study on. We've had this discussion before. . . . I know it's important.
I know you're worried. Don't . . .
Yes . . . Yes . . . I know. . . . I know. . . .
Yes. Excuse me, Mom, there's a guy
pointing a pistol at my head . . . I
think he wants a room. Wait! Don't
call the police! (hits receiver) Mom?
(hangs up) Merde!

END OF SCENE

We now have the public self and the private self on tape. Are they the same person? View the scenes again. Does the public self show elements of the private one? We behave differently for different people and situations, but the actor must not change the primal elements of the character. This person basically has stayed the same from a very early age. The nuances of change should not be jarring. Though subtle variations give a character depth and interest, they can be achieved only when the actor creates a solid foundation.

Don't Wait for Magic

Critics often say, "The actor hadn't found the character." The phrase usually results when the actor looks for the character during a perfor- mance. What we're left with is a series of interesting vignettes, schizophrenic rambling in which the actor fails to achieve a coherent persona. Relying on the gods or muses to find character almost always results in a performance in which the character changes from scene to scene.

I can hear that stage actor yell from the back of the room, "What's wrong with that? It's kind of exciting!" Yes, there is a play repertoire in which this method might be acceptable. There are some plays in which the characters are symbols or live in a manner far removed from normal psychological drives. Once again I remind you, we are applying our acting methods to film and television. I assure you that avant garde is a rare animal in this world.

When you do plays you say to yourself . . . OK, I'm six feet tall, have dark hair, bad teeth, bunions, whatever. But every time I see my self on film, I think . . . Oh my God, that's all!

Annette Benning

If we accept that film creates a more credible reality than stage, it is logical to expect a very realistic character. You'll notice that I didn't say *truer*, because what is truer for stage or film has nothing to do with the comparative quality of either. They simply are different.

An actor on stage is never alone. Even in the most contemplative moments, one is aware of the audience. A good actor in film allows the camera to capture the most private moments without the audience ever being aware of the acting.

When people name their favorite movie, their choice is most often predicated on their memory of the characters. The characters motivate the plot and not vice versa. It is incidents in the story that effect the change of character. This leads to another ingredient to help us find the persona. Simply put, How do the things that happen in the story affect your character, and how does your character affect the story? With the aforementioned attitudes as a guideline, you now must list the points in the story in which even the most minute changes affect the character.

To become aware of this technique, let's begin with the character you should know best, yourself.

EXERCISE 11: YOUR DAY

This is not an acting exercise, but rather a way for you to be conscious of the changes you experience in your hour-to-hour living. Keep a journal for a day. In it, list every emotional event from the time you wake up until you go to sleep. These should be short sentences that describe your feelings. Nothing, absolutely nothing, should escape. For example, "No parking spaces. I'll be late. If I had been here earlier, I'd have had a better chance of getting a space. I'm angry with those jerks who were here. I'm also angry with myself for not getting up earlier."

Videotape the reading of the journal. On playback try to determine what, if any, attitude generally prevails. Look for the shifts between good feelings and negative ones. Take particular notice of cause and effect. Are your responses what others would expect of you? Are they "normal"? It is important that you not enhance this journal in an attempt to be more interesting. If the writing becomes literary, you are defeating the purpose of the exercise.

The next part of the exercise is to become a character of your choice. The character should be involved in pretty much the same activities as you—Don't let the character become involved in a murder mystery, for example. Forget plot. Simply behave as a character in normal, everyday circumstances. Videotape at least one-half hour of yourself as this character.

Compare the "real you" journal tape with that of the character. Examine the cause-and-effect reactions with particular regard for actions.

We Are Known by the Things We Do

To play a person entirely different from yourself involves the same basic steps, but your psychological tether is much longer. The question of how the character would react has no correlation to you in similar circumstances, because you are bound by law, convention, and your personal morality. The character lives in the world the author created, in which conventional behavior may be disregarded. It is a time for invention and discovery. So many actors enjoy the challenge because it allows them to go under the text and create a subworld in which all interesting characters exist.

This is also the perfect opportunity to go overboard and make terrible choices. It is a time when stereotypes and prejudices rush to the foreground and display their comfortable wares to the innocent actor. I don't believe there has ever been an actor who hasn't succumbed at times. What is most important is to keep a link, a thread, to your own reality.

An example is Anthony Hopkins's portrayal of Hannibal Lecter in *The Silence of the Lambs*. Here was a cannabalistic monster whose sense of humor gave him enough humanity to compel the audience almost to like him. It was that bit of Anthony Hopkins in there that made the character more complex, more human.

> *There was nothing new I would experience as a character that I had not already experienced as a 35-year-old. . . . The one fundamental thing that I carry with me as an actor in every part I play is that at any moment, you are re-creating. There is something you want. Once you know what, you just call on your memory bank and you've got it.*
>
> *Sidney Poitier*

Don't worry if the memory bank is only 18 years old. You'll undoubtedly play people your own age, so use what's there and continue to make deposits.

> *I try to find the opposites. When I am playing a king, I find the man. When I play a man, I find the king. If there are a lot of black moments, I find the humor.*
>
> *Derek Jacobi*

The Dilemma

The creation of a unique character in film and television presents a unique dilemma. Some very good actors who have succeeded in such creation have found themselves repeating the role in film after film. A young leading man with a wide range of acting talent soon became a brand name by virtue of creating an indelible character. The actor's name was Peter Lorre. In modern films I think of Harry Dean Stanton, who seems to have cornered the market on the existentialist drifter.

How does this affect an actor contemplating a career in film? My conjecture is that habits are easily formed when the positive response to something you do is overwhelming. The desire to do it again is quite compelling. If you learn the right tricks and see the incredible results, you'd certainly be tempted to use them again. Many actors have built careers and fortunes on such stuff and won Academy Awards. Yet there is a very good reason to be cautious.

If you accept the fact that casting in film and television follows a realistic path, that is, that you will be cast according to age, type, and image, should you then develop yourself as a character? I think not. The difficulty becomes how to persuade the people who cast you because you are you of the necessity to create a new persona: the character.

If you go too far they might object with the rationale that they would have cast someone like that if they had wanted such a person. The reason you are there usually means they saw your picture and were looking for someone like you. Yet as a creative actor, you don't want the character to just be you.

In real life we acquire manners, gestures, and attitudes that differentiate us from others. They are the habits that either endear us to people or stimulate negative reactions. Many times I have heard people remark that certain actors are quite dull when not performing. They are nonverbal and offer little to the social group. Elia Kazan remarked that Robert De Niro found release and fulfillment in becoming other people. If you have ever seen an interview with Mr. De Niro, you've recognized one of those actors who doesn't feel comfortable talking about himself or his technique.

Does this mean that you should repress your own personality to allow room for the character? I don't believe that's necessary. I strongly caution you, however, not to allow your idiosyncrasies to dominate role after role. It may lead to financial rewards but artistically can be boring and frustrating. The problem with this kind of success is that once it is achieved, it's difficult to escape. (I know, you'll cry on the way to the bank.) The same problem lies with actors in television series. Once the public becomes accustomed to an actor as a certain character because of time and repetition, it is almost impossible for the actor to play other parts.

When you think about it, the same condition existed long before television. Two actors come to mind: Jimmy Stewart and Bette Davis. In spite of their strong personalities, they both managed to become the character in their films because of their equally strong talent. However, both defined their image so indelibly on the public, no matter what role they played, there still remained a certain trademark effect.

The creation of character emanates from within—from meticulous study of details, minutiae, body language, and voice. But two other elements also contribute. They are costume and make-up. Whether you are an actor who works from the outside in (like Dirk Bogarde) or the opposite (like a method actor) or use any of the varied techniques, I believe that make-up and costume psychologically will assist you.

Time, the nemesis of film and television acting, always rears its ugly head. Don't expect long, searching conversations with the director concerning character. Read the script, do your homework, and bring something to contribute. If you do this in an intelligent, deliberate way, chances are you'll have something good.

I search for the highest possible dramatic conflict in the scene. You mustn't start climbing walls just because that would be exciting. That's like having a bunch of different size pearls, each one beautiful, but they won't string together to make a necklace. I'm interested in how a character could behave, not in how he should behave. Then, if I can find a legitimate way to make that exciting, I'll push for that.

Jack Lemmon

Actors should make a choice. Even if they make the wrong choice, it doesn't matter. You can change that, give them something else to play. They should decide the character's intention in the scene: that is what the character wants and how they intend to go about getting it. My approach is to work through actions . . . that is, every actor at every moment has an intention. The emotion is a byproduct.

Glenn Jordan

Tics and Tricks

A lazy actor can achieve a distinctive character quickly simply by adding on a distinguishing physical action. We've all seen movies and television shows in which we become fascinated by an actor who chooses to make a facial tic every ten seconds. This "adding on" technique has one main drawback. The mannerism seems to exist on its own rather than becoming an organic part of the character.

You must be able to define some event in the history of the character to be able to defend your choice of a distinctive mannerism.

Habitual behavior means just that. Sometime in the past, the character began to act in specific ways when presented with specific situations. The question to answer is, Why? When you stir your coffee, where do you put the spoon? OK, you don't drink coffee, or you don't use sugar. Take any mundane action that occurs every day and think about why you perform that action time and time again. It may be small and insignificant, but it defines a part of you. The character has similar traits, and it's up to the actor to find them.

Most directors will just let you do it. They don't give an actor a bunch of ideas first. They let the actor do it his way first. Then maybe the director wants to try something. If you feel it's silly, you say, "Ah, what do you want to do that for!" Maybe what they want you to do makes you feel uncomfortable. Well, just the reason it's uncomfortable may be the reason that it's good. The point is, sometimes when you're tentative about something, your tentativeness works for another reason. . . . Many times people are talking to people and doing one thing, and they're thinking another—and it shows.

Robert De Niro

I asked Jack Lemmon what he expected from a director.

A lot of things. Really good directors work the same in a lot of ways and at the same time they are all unique. But no matter what, you have to trust them. Unfortunately this trust can be misplaced, and there you are, on the screen, months later, quite dissatisfied with your work. The good director also must have a trust in you. There is nothing more frustrating than to come on the set with a good idea and the director won't even listen. A good director is open to ideas and listens to them diplomatically even when he has no intention of using them. There wasn't a time in seven pictures when I couldn't tell Billy Wilder that I had a great idea. And he'd say, "Don't tell me . . . show me."

Jack Lemmon

This is an important clue: *Don't tell me, show me.* It goes back to making choices and doing it. Mr. Lemmon went on to say that Billy Wilder, after watching the great ideas, more often than not, gently asked to see the scene again, with his own suggestions.

EXERCISE 12: ONE'S MIND IS ELSEWHERE

                         ONE
        I know what you're saying. It's
        happened to me.

                         TWO
        Well, it's not a pleasant experience.

                         ONE
        No, it wasn't.

                         TWO
        When did it happen to you?

                         ONE
        I don't remember . . . a year ago.
        Maybe two.

                         TWO
        You're not good on dates.

                         ONE
        No.

                         TWO
        I am. I remember all the important
        dates. I remember silly dates.

                         ONE
        Look . . . can we change the subject?

                         TWO
        Sure.

                         ONE
        Thanks.

                         TWO
        Weather.

                         ONE
        Whether or not.

                    TWO
No . . . I meant weather . . . rain,
snow . . .

                    ONE
Sleet . . .

                    TWO
Fog.

                    ONE
Earthquakes . . .

                    TWO
I don't think that earthquakes can be
in the weather category.

                    ONE
Oh.

                    TWO
It's more of a disaster.

                    ONE
OK.

                    TWO
Like an avalanche. Or a rock slide.

                    ONE
It's getting pretty late.

                    TWO
I suppose. You want a lift?

                    ONE
No . . . You go on. . . . I'm just going to
sit here for a while.

                    TWO
You sure?

No answer. TWO leaves.

                              END OF SCENE

EXERCISE 13: CHOICES

Each character in the scene can be played in a variety of ways. Each couple should tape the scene at least twice, each time with new choices.

ONE enters and hands TWO a piece of paper. TWO reads the paper, then puts it down and looks at ONE.

> ONE
> Is there something wrong?

> TWO
> Maybe you should tell me that.

> ONE
> I don't know what you mean.

> TWO
> It is not the proper form. You must
> use the proper form.

> ONE
> I'm sure it's the proper form. . . . I got
> it from the office.

> TWO
> The office?

> ONE
> You're the one who sent me there.

> TWO
> No. I don't think so.

> ONE
> It was yesterday. I came to see him
> and you told me that I needed an
> entry permit. You sent me to office at
> the end of the hall. I told them you
> sent me, and they gave me this.

> TWO
> They made a mistake if what you're
> saying is true.

> ONE
> Of course it's true!

TWO
The point is that this is not the
correct form and you need the correct
form to see him. If you get the
correct form, you can see him next
week on visiting day.

ONE
Next week will be too late.

TWO
I see.

ONE
Please.

TWO
It isn't my fault you got the wrong
form. You come in here and expect
me to waive all of the procedures. I
didn't bring the wrong form.

ONE
Two minutes . . . just two minutes. No
one will know.

TWO
Leave.

ONE
To make it easier for you.

TWO
You cannot stay here. Leave.

ONE begins to leave.

TWO
If I let you in, they would kill me.

ONE
I know. . . . I'm sorry.

TWO
You come in asking for your favors
because you love someone, and you
don't think that you could kill someone else if you are obliged.

>   ONE
> I'm truly sorry. Maybe I'll try to get
> the proper form today. Maybe they'll
> let me in for the afternoon session.

>   TWO
> No.

>   ONE
> If I explain I got the wrong one . . .

>   TWO
> It wasn't wrong.

>   ONE
> What did you say?

>   TWO
> The form you brought was right.

>   ONE
> But . . . I don't understand. You
> said . . .

>   TWO
> No matter what you brought, it would
> be wrong. There is no right form for
> you.

>   ONE
> Why? Why this charade? You could
> have told me this yesterday. Damn
> you!

>   TWO
> Quiet! I have already put myself in
> enough danger by telling you this.
> Now you must leave. Please.

One starts out.

>   ONE
> I want to thank you.

ONE leaves.

>   TWO
> Thank you?

                                    END OF SCENE

What does One want? How does One go about getting this? What does Two want? Where is the change, and how does it affect the characters? Verbalize the difference, and see if the group agrees. Does the body language reveal character?

It's been said there really is no such thing as character. Habitual behavior or action delineates what we are. The problem for the actor is defining the habitual behavior. The philosophers and theorists of acting can call things what they want. An actor is a pragmatist who, with only the written word, must be able to bring someone to life. The film actor must be able to portray that life truthfully whenever the director says, "Action!"

I don't believe there is a married person in this world who hasn't heard the phrase, "It's not what you said, it's the way you said it." For me, this is a succinct definition of what an actor does. Like the married couple, you must live and react in the subtext. Then, and only then, do we see the behavior we call character.

Films to Study

Marriage of Maria Braun. Directed by Rainer Werner Fassbinder. Hanna Schygulla's portrayal of a woman's rise to power is memorable.

Death in Venice. Directed by Luchino Visconti. Dirk Bogarde speaks very little in this slow-moving but fascinating film.

Dog Day Afternoon. Directed by Sidney Lumet. Al Pacino as the hoodlum revels in the spotlight.

Pele the Conqueror. Directed by Billie August. Max von Sydow won an Oscar nomination for this role.

Thelma and Louise. Directed by Ridley Scott. Geena Davis and Susan Sarandon in their scenes together show rare perfection in the connection between two characters.

On the Waterfront. Directed by Elia Kazan. The entire cast defines ensemble acting: Marlon Brando, Eva Marie Saint, Karl Malden, Lee J. Cobb, and Rod Steiger.

Any films acted by Sir Alec Guinness, particularly *The Bridge on the River Kwai* and *Tunes of Glory*. Sir Alec's depth of character in both these films is remarkable.

Any films acted by Meryl Streep. Her technique and range is superb.

6
Focus

The Environment

Movie sets are busy places. Even when you are doing a very dramatic scene, you are aware of the camera moving, the microphone flipping back and forth to catch the dialogue, and all kinds of technical devices with people doing their jobs as you act. One flick of your eyelid that acknowledges any of this activity ruins the scene.

An actor must separate the brain into two parts. One part makes note of the technical requirements. The other ignores them completely and creates. When your focus throughout the performance is perfect, you achieve a sensibility in which the audience loses you, the actor, the person, and avidly accepts the character. It is then that the audience cries, laughs, exalts, lives, and dies with the character you have created.

The Love Scene

There is nothing more difficult in film and television acting than a love scene. It is nearly always filmed in extreme close-up, which necessitates complicated, technical camera preparation. To say that we all are most vulnerable in this kind of scene is an understatement. From puberty on, love, the idea of love, the ramifications of love, and most of all, the physical and psychological aspects of love play a very important part in our lives.

Every so often you read that an actor dismisses questions regarding love scenes with the casual remark, "All in a day's work." You may believe that, if the actor has made a lot of films with a lot of love scenes, but even then, I have serious doubts.

Let's forget the technical necessities and concentrate on the fact that it's a love scene. You have these two large faces, inches away from each other, expressing some of the most personal human emotions. There on the set, ten inches from their lips, is a monster camera lens. Behind the lens is a camera operator, a director, a sound technician holding a microphone six inches above the couple, and farther back, about thirty more people in the crew.

All eyes focus on the actors.
They are in bed, seminude or, in some cases, nude.
Each actor is extremely nervous.
The director is nervous.
The script is clichéd. How can it be otherwise?
The camera can detect a lie in an instant.

It's a terrible situation. The actors are speaking tender words of love, and the results could be disastrous. For some reason, a love scene that goes wrong on the screen sends audiences into nervous giggles. As some critics put it, there must be chemistry between the actors.

The fact is, film and television love scenes are much more intimate than love scenes in plays. They're also more difficult to perform, yet actors put off rehearsing them fully until the camera is rolling. I'm not advocating sloppy, wet kisses in rehearsal. I am suggesting that the actors lie close together in an embrace, faces an inch or two apart, and run lines before the scene is shot.

The actors must familiarize themselves with the situation so that when it comes time to shoot, they've gone through the nervous reactions and are ready to do the scene.

Because a filmed love scene demands reality, many are shown with the actors nude or seminude. If this is the case, the actors should discuss their feelings about this and try to create a common bond regarding the situation. Let's face it, they're the only two people on the set without clothes. The actors should be reassured that great pains are taken to respect their propriety. In fact, I've never seen crews more unobtrusive than on the days this kind of scene is shot.

One hint for the actor: Use gum or mouth spray, and don't eat onions, garlic, or spicy food before the scene. Stories are told with relish about actors who violated this rule.

EXERCISE 14: THE LOVE SCENE

The actors are in each other's arms, very close. The camera and camera operator are as close as possible, an extremely close shot of the faces. Someone plays the director and another the sound technician; each is within three feet of the actors. The rest of the class focuses close attention on the actors. The idea is to make them as uncomfortable as possible. The scene must be played very slowly. The actors remain in one position.

ONE

I love you.

                    TWO
I love you, too.

                    ONE
I love your smile.

                    TWO
I love your nose.

                    ONE
My nose?

                    TWO
And the way you talk.

                    ONE
You're crazy.

                    TWO
You love a crazy person.

                    ONE
I can't believe this happened to us.

                    TWO
I knew it would.

                    ONE
You did?

                    TWO
It was karma.

                    ONE
Karma?

                    TWO
You don't know what karma is?

                    ONE
Uh uh.

                    TWO
Well, karma is . . . I can't believe you
don't know this.

                    ONE
Hey, don't get mad.

                    TWO
          I'm not mad . . . I'm just a little
          amazed.

                    ONE
          I love you.

A long pause.

                    ONE
          I really love you.

                    TWO
          I love you, too.

                                        END OF SCENE
_____

I threw in the change of direction for fun. I'm sure there were enough giggles just getting into position. It's either that or becoming very, very serious about the scene with much discussion of where the hands go, whose nose is where, and solicitous questions about your fellow actor's comfort.

A love scene is difficult on all levels. For the actor, the trouble is these scenes evoke laughter if they aren't played well. You can succeed on a scale of 1 to 10 with any other kind of dramatic scene, but a love scene is either a 10 or a dismal failure.

A love scene on stage can be quite poetic. The use of language in plays is often praised by critics and accepted by the audience. But something happens to those lines when then are transformed to film. They become corny, theatrical. A love scene in a film involves naturalistic language and, if the scene is written well, little dialogue. One expects stage actors to tell us their intimate thoughts. Film actors (with a good script) keep quiet and show us.

> *I use the people I'm working with to generate emotion. In* A Hatful of Rain *I was supposed to be in love with Eva Marie Saint. I found there was so much of her that was easy to love, so I just used that. Then heightened it.*
>
> *Don Murray*

There are stories about actors who conducted steamy on-screen romances but disliked each other in real life. I won't mention any names, but see *An Officer and a Gentleman* for an example. It doesn't matter how you generate the emotion. It only matters that it's real. Unfortunately, many times a failed love scene is not an acting problem but a life problem. Actors protect themselves from romantic love in their personal lives for all kinds of reasons.

Unfortunately, the negative reasons are not easily disguised. The answer is to use any kind of love as your image—love of someone in your family, your best friend, your dog, your car . . . whatever—and use that image for your love scene.

Substitution is a tried-and-true acting technique, used for all kinds of situations. For an actor who has trouble filming a love scene, it is one of the best solutions. For an experiment, try one of the images of nonromantic love just listed when you do your love scene and see if the substitution is detected.

In any kind of scene, the problem with focus is that it can be easily faked. In an exercise in which you read a dramatic scene while others try to distract you, I guarantee that you would be able to continue without paying heed to any of the distractions. Simply set your mind to it and resolutely ignore the distractions. That is not dramatic focus.

Just as you can pretend to listen, you can also pretend to focus. For example, at certain moments an actor seems to be in a role and at moments out of the role. From scene to scene there are fluctuations that have nothing to do with character development. Even within a scene, there seems to be no organic center, no continuity.

In all sorts of endeavors, athletic, academic, or artistic, one often hears someone say, "I can't understand it. I had it down perfectly at home. It was great at practice." Athletes call it *choking*. Whatever you call it, it happens to everyone at some time. The solution for actors is to recognize the symptoms and have a technique strong enough to overcome them.

Some actors, once they get into character for a movie, stay in that mode twenty-four hours a day. They eat, sleep, and live the role. If they feel this is necessary that certainly is their prerogative. I prefer that actors develop a method to call upon their characters at will and live the rest of their day-to-day existence as themselves. Pity the friends of an actor who lives the role when the character is a serial killer.

To help you detect and correct lack of focus, which is an elusive acting fault, perform the following exercise.

EXERCISE 15: FOCUS

This exercise is conducted in three parts and is shot on three separate occasions, at least a day apart. Do not view the scene until all segments have been taped. (It is best if all segments are shot on the same tape.)

Part 1

ONE and TWO sit side by side, close together, facing forward.
They are admiring a view.

                    ONE
I love this time of day.

                    TWO
Yeah.

                    ONE
Yeah?

                    TWO
So . . . what's on your mind?

                    ONE
I thought we came up here to admire
the view.

                    TWO
Oh.

                    ONE
You always think there's something
behind everything.

                    TWO
I'm paranoid. OK? Now that we've got
that settled, let's just look at the view.

                    ONE
Well, it's true isn't it?

                    TWO
Whatever you say.

                    ONE
It would be nice if you didn't
patronize me.

                    TWO
I didn't mean to. . . . The view is nice.

                    ONE
OK.

                    TWO
What do you want?

                              END OF PART ONE

Part 2

> ONE
>
> I don't want anything.

> TWO
>
> Fine.

> ONE
>
> I say we admire the view.

> TWO
>
> Fine.

A long silence.

> ONE
>
> I know you lied to my father.

> TWO
>
> You can see the shoreline.

> ONE
>
> The question is why.

> TWO
>
> The waves breaking . . .

> ONE
>
> Why would you lie?

ONE looks at TWO. TWO turns to meet the gaze and smiles.

END OF PART TWO

Part 3

> TWO
>
> Is this a theory you have?

> ONE
>
> No. It's a feeling.

> TWO
>
> A feeling.

                    ONE
I know you.

                    TWO
I see.

                    ONE
Well?

                    TWO
So you hiked me up this mountain to
inspire my confession.

                    ONE
I'm your friend.

                    TWO
Oh?

                    ONE
I am.

                    TWO
And you think I'm a liar.

                    ONE
No.

                    TWO
Yes you do.

                    ONE
I thought you might like to tell me.

TWO turns away, looks at the view.

                    TWO
When I was a kid, I used to count the
seconds between the waves breaking.
I think it averaged about four seconds. . . . (Counts) One thousand. Two
thousand. Three thousand. Four . . . I
was right.

As TWO begins counting again, we see that ONE was right about
the lie. They both share the gravity of the terrible secret.

TWO
One thousand. Two thousand. Three
thousand. Four thousand . . . (Repeat
if you wish.)

END OF SCENE

Upon completion of the third section, view the three segments together.

Does the dramatic progression flow from one section to the other? Are the actors using the same voice levels? Inflections? Nuance? Does their mood give us a sense of place? Is it a hot summer morning or a brisk fall day? Do they make us see the view? Do we feel the connection between the two throughout the sections? *Does it look as if it were shot in one long take?*

The process then is preparation (your homework) and focus, which is the ability to deliver when called upon. The popular word for it is *charisma*. Some studio executives use the phrase, "The camera loves this person." What they are describing is an actor in true focus—a person who compels one to watch.

For another exercise, take any scene and break it into three parts. Tape the parts on different days. Play them back together, and again look for that sense of continuity.

The one actor I would nominate for perfection in both characterization and focus is Marlon Brando. View *A Streetcar Named Desire* or *On the Waterfront*. Look particularly for the scenes in which Brando is listening and reacting.

EXERCISE 16: THE READING

Close-up. The actor looks to camera left, picks a spot, and holds.

ONE
I remember the place so well . . . even
though I was only five. . . . You came
around this bend in the road, and
then suddenly you could see the
village and the small harbor. The
fishing boats were in . . . it was late in
the afternoon. . . . A few tourists were
sitting at the cafe. I always looked at
them as if they were tourists and I
wasn't. Sort of a superior me against
them. Anyway, it was my village in a
way. I bet none of them had family
from there. If you looked up to the
right of the cafe and the flagpole, you

could see where my grandparents
lived. There was a huge fig tree in
the courtyard, and the roof was slate
blue. They died before I ever got to
know them. It was so quiet there.
Just the sound of the gulls and the
boats chugging in and out of the
harbor. You could smell the fresh fish
and the ocean in the morning. Sometimes I thought I'd like to live there.
But I didn't, did I? And I never went
back. I don't understand it. I really
don't.

END OF SCENE

To whom are you speaking?
Do you see the images?
Do we see them with you?
What is the speaker doing?
Do we get a sense of the character's history?

Imitation

A sure sign that focus is wavering is imitation—an acting note that belongs in all chapters. Beware of imitation. I don't mean imitating your favorite actor. I mean picking up the cadences and accents of the person with whom you're acting. The most insidious imitative process is cadence or rhythm. It's a natural thing to do. As the scene progresses, you'll find that each person begins to respond in the same amount of time. In a fast-paced comedy scene this may be fine. But it can be disconcerting in a dramatic scene, in which symmetry could easily outweigh the meaning. American actors doing Shakespeare get into poetic grooves that may have audience members tapping their feet as they wonder what the actors are saying.

Accents also are dangerous. Because actors train their ears to pick up regional accents, they sometimes lapse into one without thinking. I know a lot of actors who after spending a week in Texas or New York sound like they come from there. If you are in a scene with someone who has developed a mild accent, be aware of it and take the time to make sure you are not mimicking the other actor.

Focus stems from a feeling of confidence. Actors solid in their choices and intelligently and emotionally prepared exude something extra, something unde-finable, that compels us to watch. They are charismatic. Watching them makes us realize that acting is truly an art.

7
Comedy

The Big Difference

There is a forgiveness factor in drama that allows it to partially fail yet have a certain measure of success. People can be specific about which scenes they liked or disliked without having the whole event ruined for them.

Not so with comedy. It's a ten or zero. If you don't get laughs, you don't have a comedy. My definition of acting hell is to be performing in a play billed as a comedy, not get any laughs, and know there is another hour of play to go.

Let's look at a successful comedy. In theater, the reaction is immediate. The actor plays off the audience reactions. A good comic actor learns from each performance and enhances the part, finding laughs where there were none before.

An actor in film has no such reactions to rely on. Even if the crew members wanted to react after seeing ten rehearsals, they had better not ruin a take by laughing while cameras are rolling. Acting in a comedy is serious business, in which instinct and trust of the material and the director play important parts.

Every year we read about actors we all accept as a serious actor saying they are tired of drama and want to do a comedy. A lot of them succeed and overcome audience prejudice about their image. But a lot of them fail. Lousy script, bad director, horrible casting—the excuses are always the same.

You Need a Sense of Humor to Do Comedy

Have you ever met anyone who admits having no sense of humor? People admit they have no ear for music. They even admit they hate dogs and children. But I have never heard anyone say, "I have no sense of humor."

The problem is defining what the phrase means. This is more difficult than it seems. For instance, when you try to analyze an audience at a play from night to night, you get a very confusing picture of what makes people laugh. On one night it howls at every line; the next night there is deadly silence. Another time it laughs at all the wrong things. You notice I keep saying *it*. That is because audiences respond as a unit, especially in comedy.

Many an actor has delivered the punch line (the one that always works), waited, and died through the silence, realizing the audience was not going to laugh. Later in the play the actor speaks a line that has never before even raised a chuckle. Wham!

The audience stops the play with its roar.

It's been said that laughter is contagious. The opposite also may be true. You show a friend a cartoon you think is hilarious and it gets handed back without a smile. Who's wrong?

If we decide that we can't define a sense of humor, how do you know if you have one? If you believe you don't, are you going to admit it? Most actors find out the hard way. They bomb in two or three comedies and make a vow to never do a comedy again. This may not be an intelligent way to make career decisions. Maybe the script was bad, the director was horrid, or. . . . A stage actor has an advantage over a film and television actor: The verdict is swift and decisive. A film and television actor won't find out whether the comedy works until months later when the picture is shown. If it's really awful, there's a chance it may become a cult classic.

You can learn techniques to alleviate the anxieties associated with performing comedy. As has been painfully shown in the past, however, there are no guaranteed results.

Comedy usually doesn't work if the actor thinks he's funny. Really lasting comedy is usually unconscious as far as the character is concerned. They don't think it's funny. You think it's funny. . . . In film, you cannot wait for the laugh because you're sure it's there. Nobody knows if it's there. You must play it legitimately. In Some Like It Hot *Billy Wilder gave one of the great pieces of direction in one of the greatest comedy scenes ever written. I had been out dancing with Joe E. Brown with a rose in my teeth and I'm lying in bed when Tony Curtis comes in from a date with Marilyn Monroe. I'm playing the maracas and he asks me what's up. I say I'm engaged. He says, "Congratulations, and who's the lucky girl?" Now I'm so psyched up about being a girl that I reply, "Me." Now after I say "engaged," Billy figured the dialogue would get buried with laughs, so in order to play the scene and hear the words, he devised a piece of business. I shook the maracas between lines and danced and sang like the happy girl I was. The spaces were filled with funny business, the scene held, and you could hear the dialogue. You have to look for a piece of business that is legitimate.*

In Mr. Roberts we had another kind of situation. When Ensign Pulver blows up the laundry and is covered with soap lather . . . We shot the scene three different ways. First, we did it like it was in the play, and I didn't wait for laughs. I filled in with blowing soap bubbles and reacting to the stuff, etc. We then did two other versions. One a little slower and the next even slower. In other words, we were giving the audience space to laugh. The last two versions bombed in previews and we went back to the legitimate one. The audience may have missed some lines, but it worked.

Jack Lemmon

I can think of three more recent examples of the actor playing it straight and letting the comedy happen. Leslie Nielsen in *Naked Gun* thinks he's a marvelous detective. He is never aware of the mayhem he creates, nor does he react to any of it. Like Inspector Clouseau (played by Peter Sellers) in *The Pink Panther*, he is intent on doing his job. If one were to take away the sight gags and the terrible puns, Mr. Nielsen could be acting in a corny police drama.

John Cleese, in the television show "Fawlty Towers" plays an apoplectic innkeeper who misunderstands almost every situation and bungles his way through life. He is a man with a terrible disposition and a nagging wife. The humor lies in the fact that Mr. Fawlty takes life very seriously and without knowing it, creates one crisis after the other. As things grow worse they become funnier. In *Ghost*, Whoopi Goldberg creates a comic character who is closer to normal; that is, if one can count as normal a crooked, fake medium who suddenly discovers her powers are real.

Goldberg and Cleese are the sources of humor, but in different ways. We laugh *at* Basil Fawlty. We laugh *with* the medium. Even though the character of Fawlty is exaggerated, Cleese plays him seriously. It is the intensity of the character that makes him so funny. Goldberg and Nielsen do not use this wild exaggeration in their respective parts. They play the roles straight, very realistically.

If you watch closely, however, you'll see that Goldberg and Nielsen, even though they play it legit, add a certain edge to the characters. This edge makes it evident that both these actors have a good sense of humor. It shows in their performances.

We're back to that phrase, *a good sense of humor.* Imagine Robert Duvall or Robert De Niro in Leslie Nielsen's role. Now, on a one-to-one basis with their most intimate friends, both these actors may be funny, witty, but their personification, their stamp, makes it extremely difficult for the audience to accept them as comedic actors.

You might think it is the audience's fault. In some ways it is. Strong dramatic actors often are typecast by the public simply because of their intensity, their talent, and a memorable part. One strong dramatic role haunts them throughout their careers, and though they play a great variety of dramatic parts with full acceptance, as soon as they do a comedy, they are rejected in the most arbitrary fashion.

Sharing the blame with the public is the power structure of the film and television business. If you start out as an orange and are accepted as an orange, you work as an orange and are recognized as an orange. The moment you also want to be an apple, you may expect indignant cries of rejection.

The point is, you may be allowed a change or two early on, but at some time, you, or someone else, will decide whether you are a comic actor—one who can do comedy. Theater, film, and television history is full of comedic actors who have switched to drama and been accepted. The opposite is not so prevalent.

Don't Act Funny

I think the most boring thing in the world is to play results. If you play the laugh rather than the character, it never is funny.

Louise Latham

With all the danger signals flying, let's attack the deadly business of comedy. First we should agree to one basic rule. The comedy we're after is not falling-on-the-floor, gasping-for-breath humor. Let us be satisfied with the gentle smile, the audible sigh of recognition, and perhaps a chuckle or two.

Your performance may also reflect a radical change from who you really are. A lot of people don't realize their comedic talent because they never search for it. You cannot tell whether actors can do comedy by their offstage personas. Two very funny actors come to mind, Woody Allen and Steve Martin. Both men, when not performing, are very quiet and shy, nothing like their stage personas. Even when both of them entertained in nightclubs and television doing stand-up comedy, their performances were in character.

This is the time to unleash the demons of comedy that exist in your subconscious and to find a funny character.

EXERCISE 17: WOMAN'S MONOLOGUE

As in the other exercises, create the character and subtext. This time try to give the person an edge, a odd way of looking at things, an honest, but not serious portrayal. You may use any business, props, or costume.

JANE

Let me tell you about Walter. He's my third husband. Well, technically he's my second and third husband. The minister who married us was sort of defrocked about six months after the ceremony. So Walter insisted we marry again. This time we got a judge. Walter felt that no matter his morals, we'd still be legal. Walter wants everything to be just right. He craves for things to be right. Not once in our marriage has he failed to mention, whenever a train is late, that, say what you want about him, Mussolini got the trains to run on time in Italy. Then he always repeats, *Italy* with his voice in the air signify-ing a can-you-beat-that tone. In the last few years, Walter has stopped talking. He answers all questions with grunts. At meals he points to things when he wants them. The only other noise he makes is when he reads the paper. Then he punctuates the silence with occasional *Hmms.* I told him once he sounded like a Buddhist monk and he asked me why. And when I got lost trying to explain the *Hmm* and the *ohm* sounds, he turned to the sports page. Walter's in the basement. He's been there for three months. He's fixing the water heater. You may wonder how a person can exist for three months without food or water. But I don't anymore.

END OF SCENE

EXERCISE 18: MAN'S MONOLOGUE

SAM

Hon, we have to talk. Hey . . . I can't talk to you when you're washing dishes. Just sit down. Good. No, I don't mind if you iron. Just listen. I want to tell you something. On the way to work this morning, I ran a stoplight and somebody ran into the car. Nobody was hurt. We got a few hundred dollars damages. The other car just scraped the paint. Anyway, this cop shows up and asks what happened and I told the truth. Besides, there were witnesses. So I get cited for running the light and we started to talking. It seems we went to the same high school in Chicago. Now here's the crazy part. We were yakking away when all of a sudden our eyes connect and something clicked . . . Oh no . . . No! I forgot to tell you the cop was a lady.
Well . . . Hon . . . I don't like creases in the sleeves. They look tacky. Well, anyway I snapped out of it and went to work. Then I go to my usual taco stand for lunch, and there she is. The lady cop. Hon, don't start the dishes . . . please. Well, we finished lunch and went to her place. What are you doing? Hey! It's very hard to talk over the vacuum. Hon! Can you hear me? This is kind of important. I know it's weird and I can't understand it. Please turn that off! . . . Thanks. Where you going? Forget the lawn. Hon, aren't you going to say something? What do you mean, "Hooray?"

END OF SCENE

After playback, the performer and the group analyze what worked. Look for the point at which something went wrong. Did the actor recover? Humor is so delicate that one rarely comes back all the way once a line goes sour.

Try to pinpoint the minute details that made the monologues funny or not. Was the business funny? Was the character a real character? Was the character likable in spite of the lines? It is a rare audience that believes an unlikable character is funny. In spite of my description of Basil Fawlty, he was still likable. Danny DeVito's character, Louie De Palma, in the television show "Taxi" is another example of a rat whom you can't help liking.

Once again the voice from the back of the room complains, "I wasn't funny, because the script wasn't funny." It is a real possibility. For that reason, do a scene that critics, audiences, and actors have thought funny for years. Now whatever I choose, someone is not going to agree that it's funny. It is the nature of the beast.

In the real world, the actor's opinion in such matters doesn't count. If you audition and get the job, don't show up with a rewrite that sparks it up a bit. Just do it!

The same goes for the following scene. *Just do it! And make it funny!*

EXERCISE 19: SOME LIKE IT HOT

Joe and Sugar are at the beach. Joe has assumed the role of a very rich man to impress Sugar. The scene begins as she chases a beach ball and he trips her. As she falls, he lowers the *Wall Street Journal.*

> JOE
> Oh, I'm terribly sorry.

> SUGAR
> My fault.

> JOE
> You're not hurt, are you?

> SUGAR
> I don't think so.

> JOE
> I'd wish you'd make sure.

> SUGAR
> Why?

> JOE
> Because usually when people find out
> who I am, they get themselves a

wheelchair and a shyster lawyer and
sue me for a quarter of a million
dollars.

> SUGAR
>
> Well, don't worry. I won't sue you—
> no matter who you are.

> JOE
>
> Thank you.

> SUGAR
>
> Who are you?

> JOE
>
> Now really ...

An off stage voice calls for her.

> JOE
>
> So long.

He begins to read the paper again. She throws the ball back, then
peers around the paper, studying him.

> SUGAR
>
> Haven't I seen you some place
> before?

> JOE
>
> Not very likely.

> SUGAR
>
> Are you staying at the hotel?

> JOE
>
> Not at all.

> SUGAR
>
> Your face is familiar.

> JOE
>
> Possible you saw it in a
> newspaper ... or magazine ... *Vanity
> Fair*

> SUGAR
>
> That must be it.

                    JOE
        Would you mind moving just a little?
        You're blocking my view.

                    SUGAR
        Your view of what?

                    JOE
        They run up a red and white flag on
        the yacht when it's time for cocktails.

                    SUGAR
        You have a yacht?

She turns and looks seaward at half a dozen yachts of different
sizes bobbing in the distance.

                    SUGAR
        Which one is yours—the big one?

                    JOE
        Certainly not. With all that unrest in
        the world. I don't think anybody
        should have a yacht that sleeps more
        than twelve.

                    SUGAR
        I quite agree. Tell me, who runs up
        that flag—your wife?

                    JOE
        No, my flag steward.

                    SUGAR
        And who mixes the cocktails—your
        wife?

                    JOE
        No, my cocktail steward. Look, if
        you're interested in whether I'm
        married or not—

                    SUGAR
        I'm not interested at all.

                    JOE
        Well, I'm not.

> SUGAR
>
> That's very interesting.

Joe resumes reading the paper.

> SUGAR
>
> How's the stock market?

> JOE
>
> Up, up, up.

> SUGAR
>
> I'll bet just while we were talking,
> you made like a hundred thousand
> dollars.

> JOE
>
> Could be. Do you play the market?

> SUGAR
>
> No—the ukelele. And I sing.

> JOE
>
> For your own amusement?

> SUGAR
>
> Well, a group of us are appearing at
> the hotel. Sweet Sue and Her Society
> Syncopators.

> JOE
>
> You're society girls?

> SUGAR
>
> Oh yes. Quite. You know—Vassar,
> Bryn Mawr. We're only doing this for
> a lark.

> JOE
>
> Syncopators. Does that mean you play
> that fast music—jazz?

> SUGAR
>
> Yeah. Real hot.

> JOE
>
> Oh. Well, I guess some like it hot. But
> personally, I prefer classical music.

SUGAR

So do I. As a matter of fact, I spent
three years at the Sheboygan Conser-
vatory of Music.

JOE

Good school! And your family doesn't
object to your career?

SUGAR

They do indeed. Daddy threatened to
cut me off without a cent, but I don't
care. It was such a bore—coming-out
parties, cotillions—

JOE

Inauguration balls—

SUGAR

—opening of the opera—

JOE

—riding to hounds—

SUGAR

—and always the same Four Hundred.

JOE

You know, it's amazing we never ran
into each other before. I'm sure I
would have remembered anyone as
attractive as you.

SUGAR

You're very kind. I'll bet you're also
very gentle—and helpless.

JOE

I beg your pardon?

SUGAR

You see, I have this theory about
men with glasses.

JOE

What theory?

                    SUGAR
Maybe I'll tell you when I know you a
little better. What are you doing
tonight?

                     JOE
Tonight?

                    SUGAR
I thought you might like to come to
the hotel and hear us play.

                     JOE
I'd like to—but it may be rather
difficult.

                    SUGAR
Why?

                     JOE
I only come ashore twice a day—when
the tide goes out.

                    SUGAR
Oh?

                     JOE
It's on account of the shells. That's
my hobby.

                    SUGAR
You collect shells?

Taking a handful of shells from the pail.

                     JOE
Yes. So did my father and my grandfather—we all had this passion for
shells—that's why we named the oil
company after it.

                    SUGAR
Shell Oil?

JOE
Please—no names. Just call me
Junior.

END OF SCENE

This scene could be called broad comedy. It is very close to skit comedy, in which the sense of reality is enhanced. Both Joe and Sugar are playing roles in the scene. That is, each is pretending to be something he or she is not. The comedy from the scene depends on the actors' delivering the lines seriously. That is, there should be no attempt to be funny. In the movie, Tony Curtis chose to do the scene as Cary Grant, and Marilyn Monroe played it innocent and awed. The problem with broad comedy is that if you go too far, the characters become cartoons and less than credible.

In acting comedy, you must maintain a certain charm, a warmth, that allows the audience to recognize the genre, forgive the occasional excess, and participate with you in the fun. In short, you must enjoy the process and let it show.

There are a couple of wordplay spots in the scene that are tried-and-true comedy-writing devices. One is as follows:

Sugar: I won't sue you no matter who you are.
Joe: Thanks.
Sugar: Who are you?

It takes precise timing to achieve the complete reversal. Another wordplay occurs when Sugar speaks of boring parties and cotillions and Joe replies "inauguration balls" and so forth. The writers use this device again when Sugar is curious about whether Joe is married. This demands a rhythm whereby each character seems to be caught up in a kind of doggerel. You must look for these writing tricks in broad comedy scenes. You must also make a variety of subchoices throughout the scene. That is, don't rely on the lines for the humor; look for a variety of feelings to influence your delivery. *A comedic character can be just as complex as a dramatic one.*

The next exercise is more subtle, less funny, and easier to play. The previous scene needs laughs to make it succeed. The following scene, less broad, settles for knowing grins.

EXERCISE 20: SUNDAY

ONE enters. TWO is reading the paper.

>   ONE
> I just love Sunday.

>   TWO
> Yeah.

>   ONE
> Did you hear me?

>   TWO
> You love Sunday.

>   ONE
> I can tell by the sound of your voice
> that you do too.

A long silence.

>   ONE
> I don't see what's so terribly wrong
> about saying that I love Sunday.

>   TWO
> I didn't say it was wrong. Can you
> manage to love Sunday without
> making a big deal out of it?

>   ONE
> I'm not making any big deal out of it.
> I would just like a response when I
> say something.

>   TWO
> Response? Who are you talking to?
> Response? Is this the gas company
> representative? Your response to the
> letter of the fifth was . . .

>   ONE
> Shut up!

>   TWO
> Let me read the paper and you'll not
> hear another word.

A long silence.

> ONE
> I like Sundays. I prefer Sundays
> when it rains or snows. I like to
> make a bowl of chili and look out the
> window. Maybe build a fire . . .

A look from TWO.

> ONE
> Definitely build a fire.

> TWO
> Prefer? Did you say "prefer"?

> ONE
> I may have. . . . It's a word that I may
> use. I know the word. Let's, for
> argument's sake, and I'm sure that's
> a condition you most enjoy, let's just
> say that I said "prefer." In fact,
> now that you mention it, I did say
> "prefer." Your response was correct.
> . . . I said "prefer."

> TWO
> You talk like a professional service
> person. "Response." "Prefer." They're
> prissy little words.

> ONE
> "Prissy" is a prissy little word.

> TWO
> It's one you don't hear from an AT&T
> operator. I talk like a human being,
> not a robot.

A silence.

> TWO
> I'm sorry.

> ONE
> Yeah?

TWO
I am. . . . No excuses.

ONE
I takes so little to set you off.

TWO
You push the right buttons.

ONE
So it's my fault.

TWO
No.

ONE
"No" means "yes."

TWO
"No" means "no."

ONE
I prefer your response to be truthful.

TWO
Let's forget it. Please?

ONE
OK.

TWO
Actually, I love Sunday too.

ONE
Don't just say that to make me feel
good.

TWO
If I said I love the frigging day, I
meant that I love it. Don't be telling
me what I love and what I don't love.
Accept it. I love Sunday. It's very
important for you to believe it when
I say that I love Sunday. I love it!
I love it.

ONE
Not when you say it like that!

                              TWO
                    It's the content that counts. Not how I
                    say it. Besides, I said it with all my
                    heart and soul. Now let's read the
                    Sunday paper and shut up before I
                    change my mind.

A long silence.

                              ONE
                    I think it's about to rain.

                              TWO
                    You're right.

                              ONE
                    How about a bowl of chili?

                              TWO
                    Sounds good.

                                        END OF SCENE

The *Some Like It Hot* scene could never play as drama. "Sunday" can. What are the main elements of humor in the scene? Could it be the absurdity of the argument? If you treat the argument as a symbol of deeper emotions between the two, you have a very unfunny scene. If you accept the scene for what it is, a silly argument between two rational people, it may play as comedy.

The problem with comedy scenes on playback is that after you've viewed the second or third version, the reactions begin to fizzle. It is the same thing on the set as you perform the scene a dozen times. The edge is gone, and you panic. This usually triggers a dangerous response from the actor: radical changes in choices, new, broader business, mugging, ad-libbing, playing to the camera instead of the other actor. *All deadly.*

You must trust the material. No one is suggesting that on repeated takes you shouldn't find fresh ideas, nuances, or small variations. The caution is not to mistake normal feelings of losing the humor and overreact. If it worked the first and second times, chances are it will work on take eleven.

The key to comedy acting is credibility. You must not think that you as the character are funny. Look at *Some Like It Hot*. Jack Lemmon as the character truly believes that he is a woman and engaged to a very rich man. His exuberance, coupled with Tony Curtis's disbelief, makes the scene hilarious. If, for a moment, Lemmon's character had revealed that it was a put-on, the scene would have failed.

Films to Study

Some Like It Hot. Directed by Billy Wilder. Magnificent ensemble comedy. This is broad comedy with sight gags and jokes. Once the tone is set, the audience accepts the incredible happenings.

Bringing Up Baby. Directed by Howard Hawks. Sophisticated comedy deftly done by Cary Grant and Katharine Hepburn. Note the restaurant scene in which she rips her dress. Terrific blocking and business. Who says you can't have a touch of slapstick in sophisticated comedy?

All of Me. Directed by Carl Reiner. Steve Martin's struggle with himself is a little broader than in the other films mentioned, but it is a great example of comedic body language.

Father of the Bride. Directed by Vincente Minnelli. Splendid comedy ensemble acting.

Father of the Bride. Directed by Charles Shyer. This remake plays very well. Except for the mugging exaggeration of Martin Short, the cast plays it straight.

Television Show to Study

"Monty Python's Flying Circus." From the ridiculous to the silly, the entire troupe performs the sketches with serious fervor. Quite often they parody officious government or business officials or comment on the modern human condition. No matter how broad the comedy, the actors are very character orientated.

8
Situation Comedy

History

From vaudeville, burlesque, stage reviews, and some musicals emerged a style of acting called *sketch comedy*. A sketch was a short piece of material, usually no more than seven or eight minutes. The actors portrayed broad stereotypes. They waited for the laughs, took pies in the face, did pratfalls, and played directly to the audience. Nothing was taboo. The best sketch comics went on to become television stars in the infancy of television, when variety shows were popular. Such people as Jimmy Durante, Eddie Cantor, Ed Wynn, and Milton Berle were some of the first people to headline their own TV shows.

Shows such as "The Carol Burnett Show" and "Rowan and Martin's Laugh In" featured this kind of comedy. After that, "Saturday Night Live" and "Monty Python's Flying Circus" carried on the tradition. But the single most important offspring of this sketch brand of humor is the situation comedy.

In situation comedy continuing characters execute a "book" show, that is, a show with a story line. Because situation comedies are a leading source of employment, it's a good idea to examine how they work from the actor's point of view.

If there is one word to describe the difference between acting for situation comedy and acting in film and long-form television comedy (movies, teleplays) I nominate *exaggeration*. In chapter 7 I suggest giving an edge to a character. In sitcom, you can give a character two edges and not be afraid of going over.

Every sitcom character is a bit of a caricature. On "The Mary Tyler Moore Show," Mary Richards worked in a TV newsroom as co-producer of the nightly news. She lived in a nice apartment and had "real" problems. Her boss, Lou Grant, played by Ed Asner, was the news director. His job was to get the news on the air and to manage the diverse group of newsroom employees. By far, Mary and Lou were the straightest, closest to normal characters on the show. But neither of them would put up with Ted Baxter, the egocentric anchorman, for a moment if they were to play it realistically.

The Ted Baxter character necessitated acting adjustments on the part of Moore and Asner. The newsroom became sort of a newsroom, but more like a theatrical set. The desks and typewriters were props. On this set Mary and Lou interacted with the other people in the cast. The other characters either set up or participated in the jokes. Though the jokes emanated from our knowledge of the characters, you can be sure they were jokes.

In situation comedy, scripts are carefully crafted so that laughs come with precise regularity. Three or four jokes a page is the general rule, which means three or four jokes a minute. To assure the success of this formula, the studio audience's reactions are reinforced with a laugh track. It is essential for the actor to realize this for one reason. *The pace of sitcom acting is regulated by the number of jokes on the page.*

A Unique Arena

In drama or straight comedy, you can, by virtue of the script, prepare and deliver lines without regard to external ideas of pace. You create an inner logic that allows the viewer to participate with you in the thought process. In chapter 7 I discuss not waiting for laughs, because there is no guarantee they will come. Not so with sitcoms.

You wait. Wait for the laugh. If there is even a glimmer of a laugh, you can be sure it will be augmented in edit. Lines are not allowed to die. This practice is much abused. Too often a character says hello and gets a huge laugh.

Most sitcoms are performed in front of a live audience. (This is usually announced on the air so the viewer, I suppose, won't think it is a dead audience.) The reason is simple. The actors can measure their performance according to the reactions of the people. They tape two performances. One is called the *dress*, and the other is the taped show. Editors cut together these two performances for the aired version.

Sitcoms always use multiple camera techniques. One camera is on the master, or long shot. Two other cameras cover over-the-shoulder close-ups. A fourth camera may isolate only the star. This multiple camera setup makes it imperative for the actors to hit their marks. If you're off by half a foot, you can be covering another actor's close-up.

The successful shows rely on our familiarity with the characters to get laughs. The jokes are based on prejudicial knowledge. Inferior shows go for gags for their own sake. Herein let's deal with acting for shows that are well written, clever, and character orientated.

Your Bit Part on "Cheers"

"Cheers," one of the most successful shows in the history of television has a cast of characters who are well embedded in the American TV psyche. An episode comes up in which the bar sink is stopped up, and someone is needed to play a plumber, a five-line part. The situation is that it is the plumber's first job and he or she is very nervous. Sam Malone (played by Ted Danson) notices the plumber's shaking hands. The rest of the formidable cast is present, all making comments and offering advice.

You are in the midst of people who have done show after show for five years. It's time for you to read for the part. What do you do?

1. You are not playing a plumber—you are playing an idea of what a plumber is. You need not do any research about what plumbers do in such a situation. In fact, it's best not to know anything about plumbing at all.

2. With absolutely no skill or knowledge, your intention is to fix the sink.

3. You do not want anyone to know this is your first plumbing job and that you are extremely nervous. (You also might not want them to know it's your first sitcom job.)

4. Use the fact that the cast members all know each other and you are an outsider. (Make your nerves work for you.)

5. Make the plumber a character in a sitcom. That means exaggerate the walk, the talk, and the use of props. When you read for a part in a sitcom, don't be afraid to exaggerate. Not doing enough will seldom get you hired. Directors like the idea that you're willing to let it all hang out.

6. Know the show. A plumber on "Cheers" is different from a plumber on "Roseanne." Analyze the comedy style of the show, and gear your performance to that style. For example, on "Roseanne," Roseanne delivers most of the jokes. The other characters play straight—they set up the situation for the punch line. On "Cheers," every cast member has a punch line at one time or another. That ensemble feeling can apply to a bit player coming in for one scene.

7. However you can, find out about the star's idiosyncrasies, working habits, and peeves. Sitcom filming involves a great deal of pressure. Lines are changed constantly. Ratings may be down that week, so the network executives lurk, making the star nervous. The point is that something as simple as being in the line of sight of the performing star as you watch a scene from the sidelines can get you fired.

SITCOM SCENE—"CHEERS"

This scene from "Cheers" with Rebecca and Sam needs no explanation. Try to play the scene with a fresh approach. Don't emulate the show.

Interior of Rebecca's apartment at night. It's late. The drapes are closed, and the only light comes from a table lamp. In the dim light Rebecca, in a stupor, is sitting alone on the couch. She wears a ratty bathrobe and slippers. She has a drink in her hand. Around her are empty liquor bottles, filled ashtrays, dirty dishes, and empty pizza boxes. The place is trashed, and so is she. We hear the sound of the doorbell; it jolts her. She moves unsteadily to answer it.

> REBECCA
> Hold your horses, I'm just putting
> down my beverage. Here I come.

She opens the door, concealing herself behind it.

> REBECCA (CONT'D)
> Ow!

She talks to Sam through a crack in the door.

> REBECCA (CONT'D)
> Hey, you're not the pizza boy. But
> you're still cute. Come on in.

Sam enters the apartment. Because it's dark he walks right into a table.

> SAM
> Ow! How can you see anything in
> here?

> REBECCA
> I'll just open the drapes and let some
> light in here, okay?

She starts for the window, but is so unsteady she lands back on the couch.

> SAM
> Let me just get a lamp.

Sam turns a lamp on. She turns it off. He turns it on again. She turns it off.

> SAM
> "Click."

Rebecca turns on the lamp. The light causes her to blink in confusion.

> SAM
>
> Sweetheart, you're not getting your
> security deposit back on this place.

> REBECCA
>
> Come on, Sam, sit down and join me
> in a toast.

Sam crosses back to the coach.

> SAM
>
> Rebecca, are you drinking again?

> REBECCA
>
> I certainly am not. I never stopped.
> (Puts down the glass.) There, I
> stopped. (Picks it up.) Now I'm
> drinking again.

> SAM
>
> Rebecca, if something's bothering you,
> you can't use alcohol to forget it.

> REBECCA
>
> Sure I can. I've forgotten everything
> that's happened in the past two
> minutes. (Then) Hey, you're not the
> pizza boy. But you're cute.

She tries to take another drink. Sam grabs the glass out of her
hand.

> SAM
>
> Give me that.

He also scoops up as many other glasses and bottles as he can
carry.

> REBECCA
>
> Sam, you don't have to clean up. I
> just did.

> SAM
>
> It's okay. I'll just put them in the
> kitchen.

Sam crosses to the kitchen.

SAM
(Regarding glasses) Hey, these glasses
are from the bar.

Sam exits into the kitchen. Once he's gone, Rebecca goes back to
the couch, sits down, and notices that she's caught her hair with
the end of her cigarette. She stamps it out. Sam reenters and
joins Rebecca on the couch.

REBECCA
Well, look who's back.

SAM
Look, Rebecca, do you want to talk?
Does all of this have something to do
with your getting married. Are you
starting to get cold feet?

REBECCA
No. I'm perfectly prepared to marry
Robin and spend the rest of my life
with him. I'm just not particularly
looking forward to it.

SAM
What do you mean? All you've done
for the last two years is talk about
marrying this guy.

REBECCA
Well, Sam, it's one thing to love
somebody while they're serving time
for you. But it's another when you're
serving time with them. I mean,
there's so much of life I still haven't
tasted. After all, I've just discovered
this drinking thing.

SAM
Sweetheart, I understand the tempta-
tion. After all, I am a recovering
alcoholic.

REBECCA
I just don't think I'm ready to make a
commitment.

SAM

Hey, doubt is part of every relationship. I should know. I was divorced.

REBECCA

I drink for a couple of days; you were
an alcoholic. I'm having a little
trouble with a relationship; you were
divorced. Do you retain water in the
middle of the month, too, Sam?

SAM

I'm just trying to help you. Listen,
everybody gets cold feet before their
wedding. But it's a pretty weenie
reason to turn to alcohol.

REBECCA

Why did you start drinking, Sam?

SAM

I lost my curve ball.

REBECCA

I'm not drinking because I've got cold
feet. I'm drinking because I don't
know if I love Robin.

SAM

Oh, wow. You think you don't?

REBECCA

I don't know. I just wish I had more
time to decide what to do. Do you
think there's any chance the parole
board would keep him in prison for a
little while longer?

SAM

Rebecca, if you don't love Robin, why
don't you just back out?

REBECCA

It's that easy? I'm supposed to tell
the richest man in the world I don't
want to marry him?

SAM

He's not rich anymore, remember?

REBECCA
In that case, what's his number?

SAM
Come on, Rebecca, this is serious.

REBECCA
It's just that I keep remembering that
one time in my life I had something
so much more exciting.

SAM
Oh-boy. I think I know where this is
going.

REBECCA
Oh, God, I loved it so much, Sam. I
think about it all the time. It was so
magical, so thrilling.

SAM
I know. I know.

REBECCA
It was like every nerve ending in my
body was alive. Like my skin was
glowing. I was totally at one with
another being. Once that happens to
you, you never forget it.

SAM
Yeah, I'll never forget the night we
made love.

REBECCA
No. I'm talking about when I was ten
and won first place in the horse
show. (Realizing) But that night with
you was good, too. See, even sleeping
with you was better than Robin.

SAM
Even that.

REBECCA
So that's it . . . I don't want to marry
Robin. It's over. Well, I guess I won't
need this anymore. (Pulls a bottle out

from under a lamp) I've made my
decision. Robin is history. That feels
good. Let's celebrate.

She reaches for the bottle again. Sam grabs it.

                    SAM
That's enough of that.

                    REBECCA
You're right, Sam. There's a better
way to celebrate. Drop your pants.

                    SAM
What?

                    REBECCA
You heard me. I want you.

                    SAM
Whoa, hold on. We can't do this,
Rebecca.

                    REBECCA
Sure we can. Come on, Sam, the train
is leaving the station. All aboard.
(Makes train noises)

Sam slides away from her, but she follows.

                    SAM
I won't do this, Rebecca.

                    REBECCA
Why not, Sam?

                    SAM
First of all, you've been drinking, and
gentlemen have rules about that. And
second of all, you're repulsive right
now.

                    REBECCA
Can't take it?

                    SAM
I'm getting out of here.

REBECCA
What's your hurry? (Singing.) "We've
got tonight . . . Who needs tomorrow . . . "

SAM
Oh, no. No, honey.

REBECCA
(Screeching the high notes)
    "Let's make it last, babe . . . Let's FIII-
ND a way . . ."

Rebecca has backed Sam against the wall.

REBECCA
Sam Malone, get ready for the wildest
night of your li-i . . .

She faints forward into Sam's arms. They slide to the floor.

SAM
(Pinned under her) Oh, well, gee,
maybe I'd be more in the mood if we
washed your hair.

END OF SCENE

This scene, besides being difficult as comedy also has one of the hardest jobs
in acting: portraying a person who is drunk. If there ever was a chance of going
overboard, getting corny, and being just plain awful, it's when you have the
challenge of playing drunk. One of the clues to this difficulty is trying to do too
much at the same time.

People who are drunk stagger, slur their speech, blink their eyes, lose their
train of thought. They have a variety of characteristics that occur or stop
without reason. To play drunk, choose a predominant behavior and season it
sporadically with other impairments. Then just imagine these things and work
them ever so faintly into the fabric of the character as that person would behave
sober. In other words, don't act generically drunk. Be drunk as the character
would be. From that point you may exaggerate a bit, just a bit.

Suppose you decide to slur your words. People who are drunk hear themselves speaking naturally. Pick a sentence from the script. Take two words from
the sentence (two words with similar consonants), and make them your key

words. These are the words you'll come close to saying correctly. Pick two other words in another speech, and so on. If two don't work, pick three or four. The idea is to build a behavior slowly.

Because it is comedy, you still have to give the scene an edge. The fact is, someone who is drunk may be thought of as a pathetic and tragic figure. At one time, a person who was drunk provided comic relief in films. Modern thinking no longer finds that condition, in itself, amusing. In the foregoing scene, Rebecca does have a genuine problem, but it would be a mistake to play it so realistically as to kill the humor.

SITCOM SCENE—"SEINFELD"

There is a real challenge in doing a scene from "Seinfeld." The characters on the show are so well defined that it would be difficult to imagine anyone else in those parts. In fact, there was a "Seinfeld" episode in which the characters made a pilot segment and hired actors to portray themselves. George's whining complaints about the actor playing Kramer made for a very funny conflict.

So what does the actor do with this material? Is there a way to escape the indelible imprints of these characters? That is the challenge. Look for another way to play the scenes and tape it. Then, for an experiment, play the scene the way you'd imagine the "Seinfeld" characters would do it. Compare how the scenes work.

ACT ONE

Scene C

Interior of Jerry's apartment. Day 1.
(Jerry, George, Elaine, Kramer)
Jerry watches TV. Kramer is fiddling with the stereo.

> KRAMER
> Hey, Jerry, what's the matter with
> your stereo?

> JERRY
> I don't know. What's the matter with
> your stereo?

> KRAMER
> I traded it to Lomez for some steaks.

George enters with a camera.

> GEORGE
>
> Hey.

> KRAMER
>
> (Pressing buttons)
> This thing is busted.

> JERRY
>
> It works. Watch out. You just have to
> jiggle it with a screwdriver.

George snaps a picture.

> JERRY (CONT'D)
>
> What are you doing?

> GEORGE
>
> I met this woman who works at the
> 1-hour photo place. She's got this
> incredible smile like she's got too
> many teeth or something.

> JERRY
>
> Extra teeth, I love that look.

> GEORGE
>
> Get this, when I picked up my photos,
> she says, "I hope you got that mus-
> tard stain out of your shirt."

> JERRY
>
> What mustard stain?

> GEORGE
>
> Don't you see? She was looking at my
> pictures.

> JERRY
>
> So whatever mustard stain it was
> doesn't matter.

> GEORGE
>
> Couldn't have less relevance to the
> point I am trying to make here.

JERRY

I see. She's looking.

GEORGE

Yesss. In fact, I just dropped off a couple of rolls that were work related, and now I want her to meet some of my friends.

JERRY

So how many rolls have you been out with this girl? Sounds like it's getting serious.

GEORGE

Nah, this one is only twenty-four shots.

KRAMER

Jerry, you've got to get this thing fixed.

JERRY

They've tried to fix it, but it always comes back the same.

KRAMER

How about a refund? Would you be interested in a refund?

JERRY

I can't get a refund. The warranty expired two years ago—

KRAMER

Aahh! Would you be interested?

JERRY

How are you going—

KRAMER

Na, na, na! Would you?

JERRY

I guess I would.

                    KRAMER
Yeah.

Kramer leaves as Elaine enters.

                    ELAINE
You're not going to believe what
happened to me at the doctor's office.

                    JERRY
Not the gown again.

                    ELAINE
No. I was looking at my chart, and it
said I was difficult. What do you
think that means?

                    JERRY
It means they've gotten to know you.

                    ELAINE
And then he wrote some more stuff
on there. He didn't even look at my
rash.

                    GEORGE
So find a doctor who doesn't know
you're difficult.

                    ELAINE
C'mon. I'm not difficult. I'm easy.

                    JERRY
Why? Because you dress casual and
sleep with alot of guys?

                    ELAINE
Listen you little sh—

                    GEORGE
Smile.

They pose for a picture.

Cut to:

ACT ONE

Scene E

>   Interior of Jerry's apartment. Day 2.
>   (Jerry, George, Kramer, Mailman)
>   Special effects: Ding-dong

JERRY

>   (Answers the door)

A mailman holds a package and clipboard.

MAILMAN

>   Seinfeld? I got a package for you.
>   Sign here.

Jerry looks at the package. It is sloppily wrapped in brown
paper, electrical tape, and twine.

JERRY

>   Who's it from?

MAILMAN

>   No return address. Sign here.

Jerry looks over the package again.

JERRY

>   No return address? What if I don't
>   want it?

MAILMAN

>   Are you refusing delivery?

JERRY

>   Maybe I am.

MAILMAN

>   Why would you do that?

JERRY

>   I've never done it before.

MAILMAN

>   Why start now?

JERRY

Why not?

MAILMAN

All right.

He takes the box and exits as George enters.

GEORGE

Why did you refuse that? Everybody
loves packages.

JERRY

I don't know, it was weird. Crazy
printing, I don't know who it's from.

GEORGE

So? What did you think, it's a bomb?

JERRY

It's not totally impossible.

GEORGE

The ego on you. You think you're
bombable?

JERRY

Why can't I be bombable? I've been
on TV. I might have offended
someone.

GEORGE

Who's going to bomb you? An airline
for all those stupid peanut jokes?

JERRY

Oh, I suppose you think you're
bombable.

GEORGE

There's a couple of people who
wouldn't mind having me out of the
way.

JERRY

There's more than a couple.

George pulls out some pictures.

GEORGE
Hey, check these out. I just got them back.

JERRY
These are impressive. You don't have a Mercedes.

GEORGE
No, I just leaned up against it so it would look like mine.

JERRY
The driver seems a little put out.

GEORGE
He was fine with it. (Next picture) How about this outfit?

JERRY
Are those emeralds?

GEORGE
(Next picture) Whoa, whoa, whoa.

George shows him a picture of a nearly naked woman.

JERRY
Wow. That's a lot of skin.

GEORGE
Hey, I think that's Sheila from the photo place.

JERRY
You can barely see her face.

GEORGE
It's got to be her. She must have slipped this in.

Kramer enters.

KRAMER
Aye-ya-ya! She is brazen.

GEORGE
Photo store Sheila. It was in with my prints.

KRAMER
Well hello photo store Sheila.

GEORGE
See you later.

George starts to exit.

JERRY
Where are you going?

GEORGE
To ask her out.

KRAMER
No, no, no, no. You're not playing the game.

GEORGE
What game?

KRAMER
She goes to these lengths to entice you and your only response is, "I really like your picture, would you like to go out on a date with me, please?"

GEORGE
No good?

KRAMER
George, it's the timeless art of seduction. You've got to join in the dance. She dips, you bend. She sends you an enticing photo, you send her one right back.

GEORGE
I don't know.

KRAMER
As you know, I've always been something of a photog.

JERRY
Oh yeah, I like this idea.

Cut to:

ACT ONE

Scene H

Interior of a taxi cab. Day 2.
(George and Elaine)

> ELAINE
> And then he started writing on my
> chart.

> GEORGE
> So why don't you just get a hold of it
> and change what's in there?

> ELAINE
> You can't change your chart. It's
> your chart.

> GEORGE
> Exactly, it's your chart. I'm in and
> out of my personnel file at work all
> the time.

> ELAINE
> You are?

> GEORGE
> Hey, I've kept the same job for over
> two years. That's not luck.

> ELAINE
> Well. I've got to go back. This rash is
> definitely getting worse.

She scratches. George moves farther away.

> GEORGE
> Elaine, did you ever send a racy
> photo of yourself to anyone?

> ELAINE
> Yeah, I sent one to everyone I know.
> Remember my Christmas card?

GEORGE
Oh right. The nipple. Aside from that,
how did you feel about Kramer's
work?

ELAINE
I thought he was very professional.
He had a good concept and I thought
it was well executed.

GEORGE
So it was a good experience?

ELAINE
Yeah, I'm really glad I did it. In fact,
I liked the picture so much, I cropped
out the nipple and I'm using it for my
health club ID.

GEORGE
Nice.

It is important to remember that humor quite often reflects very serious situations. It's the actor's job to play the humor and leave the serious undercurrent to the viewer. Many sitcoms touch on serious issues, but they do it with a lot of laughs. If they didn't they wouldn't be called situation *comedies.*

The last point about this very special genre is not to adopt a superior attitude. Situation comedy is not beneath your talent. All of your classical training has not gone to the dogs. Your parents, friends, and fellow thespians will not disown you.

Sitcom acting can be a demanding and highly skilled technique. If you give it the same attention as any of the other disciplines of acting, it will be very rewarding.

Television Shows to Study

"Seinfeld"

"Cosby"

"Cheers"

"Mad About You"

"Murphy Brown"

"Coach"

"Fawlty Towers" (available on videotape)

"Roseanne"

"I Love Lucy"

"The Drew Carey Show"

Because sitcoms have the habit of disappearing, I've picked some that play
forever on the rerun stations.

9
The Close-up

Of all the techniques mentioned earlier, the close-up is the only one that is unique to film and television. I don't know who said, "the camera never lies," but whoever said it was almost right. I say "almost," because it is possible to fool the camera. Many politicians will attest to that (in private). But actors would be wise to believe the phrase. Because the close-up shot can be the most important tool, it can also be the most damaging.

From an article in the *New York Times* by Diane Ackerman:

There is a code of basic facial expressions that all humans share—happiness, anger, fear, surprise, disgust. Spontaneous, automatic, the face forms words before the mind can think them. We often rely on facial semaphore to tell us truths too subtle or shameful or awkward or intimate or emotionally charged or nameless to speak.

"*The face forms words before the mind can think them.*" What a provocative idea! It would seem to suggest that we react first on a primal level then think. Heroes who rescue babies by diving into raging waters invariably say, "I didn't have time to think."

To react purely in such a way is impossible while acting. From the text you know the words and the emotions. Though there may be some surprises in performance, they are most always in the context of the scene. No one wants to act with actors who leave the script whenever the mood hits them, yet there is a sense of danger when fresh emotional things happen and the scene breathes a life it never had before.

It's like the fast break in basketball, in which three players pass the ball back and forth with precision, and the last one shoots the basket. None of them knows when the ball is coming, yet when they get it, they respond perfectly and in so doing become part of the event that culminates in the scoring of a basket. They clap hands together and smile at their accomplishment.

The fast break is a product of training, imaging (knowing how it's supposed to look), and instinct. It is never the same, but it always has the same goal. Each player responds spontaneously within the circumscribed rules. *Acting should be that organic.*

I divide the close-up shot into two main categories—realization and change of direction.

Realization

In films and television the close-up is used to tell us important facts about character and plot. There are often wordless moments when the character realizes something and changes because of it. This might not be a distinctive acting problem for stage, but it certainly is for the camera. A film director isolates these moments in close-up, thereby creating a unique acting problem.

EXERCISE 21: REALIZATION 1

Realization is the point in the story at which things begin to add up. Instincts, the gut feelings, take over; words and logic have no meaning. It is when unbearable truths must be faced or when the sky clears and the sun shines.

Before taping, mark the points in the script at which you intend to change. The camera is on the listener in close-up. The speaker is off camera. Tape the scene without the group.

> VOICE
> I'm glad you came. I've been meaning
> to talk to you for a couple of weeks,
> but you know how busy we get at
> Christmas. . . . You're looking great
> . . . you always do. Well, I only have a
> minute. The damn store is packed,
> and we can't get any good help. Hell,
> that's not your problem. . . . Like I
> said I was meaning to call but. . . . I
> know we made some plans for the
> holiday. . . . What I didn't know at the
> time was that my ex was coming to
> town. I didn't expect it. She's [he's]
> visiting her [his] mom . . . and. . . . It's
> a family situation. I just don't think
> you'd feel comfortable. You know I
> want to be with you. . . . It's just . . .
> you know. . . . They're all sentimental
> about Christmas and how it used to

be. You know I'd much rather be with
you. . . . I would. . . . You OK? . . . I
knew you'd understand. . . . I'll call.
Hey, I'd hate to put you in that
spot. . . . I knew you'd understand. We
still have New Years Eve. I'll
call. . . . I promise.

                                    END OF SCENE

Does the tape version match the points you indicated on the script? Does the realization take time to build or do you reach the climax too early, leaving yourself nowhere to go at the end? Are you frustrated, angry, disappointed? Have you resolved to never see this person again, or will you forgive? What kind of person would do this to you? Does your response correlate with that person's behavior? Tape the person making the call. Make the lies sincere or phony. Let the audience decide.

EXERCISE 22: REALIZATION 2

The camera is on the listener. Someone you know and have loved has come back after a long time. In the past the person has not realized your love, but now you see that times have changed.

                    VOICE
I know you must think that I'm
stupid. You must have wondered what
I was doing, going here and there,
never making up my mind about
what I wanted. The years seem
wasted, but then I don't know how it
could have been different. I wasn't
such a good risk then. . . . I can't even
guarantee that now. But I do know
this . . . for all the years, no matter
what I did or where I was, I never
stopped thinking of you. I loved you
then and I love you now. And I don't
blame you if you tell me to go to hell.
But I want you to know there'll never
be another. I want you to know that
I'll love you and only you until the
day I die.

                                    END OF SCENE

Note the emotional stepping stones that take you from friendly understanding to the realization that you are loved.

Change of Direction

Whereas realization is mostly a gradual process, the change of direction can be either gradual or abrupt. The dramatic process usually makes the abrupt change of direction more interesting. The writer uses this device to stimulate the audience and to stay one step ahead of them. If dramatic writing were to follow a rigid path based on pure logic we'd have some pretty boring material.

It is the unexplained complexities of human nature that allow the writer to break a character away from the inexorable path and send the story off into new, exciting directions.

It is a lucky actor whose character is the instrument of such change. It is a dumb actor who makes change-of-direction choices when the text doesn't call for them. The snappy phrase for such behavior is, "going against the text." Most of the time it is an attention-getting device instigated by lack of real preparation and respect for the other actors and the script. The rare times this works are dangerous for actors because it may encourage them to try it again.

Changing direction is not an arbitrary way to alleviate boredom or to have fun. It should be a legitimate acting technique that is used only when the text calls for it.

EXERCISE 23: CHANGE OF DIRECTION

This is a parent-student scene. Camera focus is on the student.

> PARENT
> You packed?

> STUDENT
> You know I've been packed for days.

> PARENT
> You nervous?

> STUDENT
> A little. Hey, don't forget that check.

> PARENT
> I won't. I'll send it to the dorm.

STUDENT
I can get a job.

PARENT
I want your first year to be
smooth. . . . After that you'd better get
a job because I'm going to be broke. I
remember the first day I went away
to university.

STUDENT
You know . . . I really appreciate what
you're doing for me.

PARENT
I know.

STUDENT
Sometimes you might think that I act
like I don't. I know I drove you a
little bit crazy this year.

PARENT
What you're doing now made it all
worthwhile. I'm proud of you.

The phone rings, and STUDENT answers.

STUDENT
Hey . . . what's shaking? What?
Fantastic. No . . . I'm about ready to
leave. No . . . I made up my mind. . . .
I'll call. Hey, don't forget your old
friends. . . . I'm really jazzed for you
guys. . . . Later.

STUDENT hangs up, waits a beat, then returns to PARENT.

PARENT
What was that all about?

STUDENT
We got a record contract. I mean the
band got a contract.

PARENT
That's wonderful.

>   STUDENT
>   Yeah . . . Let's go.

STUDENT picks up bag, heads for door then stops.

>   PARENT
>   What did you forget?

A long pause.

>   STUDENT
>   Me. I almost forgot me.

>   PARENT
>   What do you mean?

>   STUDENT
>   It means I'm not going.

>   PARENT
>   It's a little late now to be saying
>   that . . . so the band got a record
>   contract. There'll be other
>   bands . . . after you graduate.

>   STUDENT
>   I'm not going because of you. I love
>   you a lot, but I can't do this for
>   you. . . . I thought I could. I almost
>   convinced myself that this is what I
>   wanted. . . . Maybe I will someday. But
>   not now . . . I'm going to play music.
>   It's something I really want to
>   do. . . . I'm sorry.

STUDENT goes to phone and dials.

>   STUDENT
>   Hey Chris . . . I changed my mind. I'm
>   not going. You haven't found a guitar
>   player yet, have you? . . . Great!

>   END OF SCENE

Change of direction scenes are mostly based on the characters' repression of what they really want. This repression manifests itself as tension. The pleasant facade of the student in the preceding scene masks this repression. But the actor must be careful that the facade itself is not so obvious that we are counting the seconds to the eruption. The Student can choose to be somewhat hostile, although the text states that the student loves the parent.

The Parent has seemed to have won a long, hard-fought battle, only to be defeated at the last moment. The Student can make several choices about how to acknowledge that.

It would be interesting to play the scene with a lot of tenderness and love, then repeat it with a more hostile edge from both people.

Find other realization and change-of-direction scenes and tape them in a similar way.

One last vital piece of advice about the close-up: This is the time, more than ever, to trust the camera. Think! Do not act. Do not calculate any facial expressions or movements—no lip pursing or blinking eyes.

Allow characters to behave as they would.

Films to Study

The Magnificent Ambersons. Directed by Orson Welles. The last scene with Joseph Cotton and Agnes Moorhead is a fine example of realization.

The 400 Blows. Directed by Francois Truffaut. The young boy never really escapes his repressive life. The last scene does offer some relief from inexorable tension. The freeze frame is so real, so poignant, you can't believe this is a movie.

Suspicion and *Rebecca.* Directed by Alfred Hitchcock. Both films illustrate a woman in emotional jeopardy who is frightened and repressed. Each film uses the emotional change at the end as the main plot point.

It's A Wonderful Life. Directed by Frank Capra. Jimmy Stewart's last scene is still one of the greatest realization scenes.

The Browning Version. The original film directed by Anthony Asquith. Watch Michael Redgrave's scene in which he realizes that his life at the school had meaning.

The Verdict. Directed by Sidney Lumet. Paul Newman's conversion from drunk to responsible lawyer is wonderful.

10

John Lithgow on Acting

John Lithgow has had a distinguished acting career in theater, film, and now television. He was nominated for an Oscar for his role in *The World According to Garp* and won an Emmy for his performance in the "Amazing Stories" series. Mr. Lithgow received another Emmy for the hit series "3rd Rock from the Sun." Mr. Lithgow was graduated from Harvard University in 1967 and was a recipient of a Fulbright scholarship. This interview was conducted in Mr. Lithgow's dressing room in Studio City, California, January 22, 1997.

Film

I think there's a great difference between movies and live television, that is, a sitcom. For one thing, the pace of doing a movie is quite slow. For this reason, there's a lot of time on the set. So I usually don't learn lines until the very day we shoot the scene. That way I try to keep them fresh. You see, in features you only shoot two or three scenes a day, and you do those scenes over and over again. So it's vital to be alive and fresh, especially at the end of the day when they do the close-ups. It's especially important at that time to be up on your game.

Even though I don't learn the actual lines, I try to have a thorough discussion with the director about the character. For instance, when Glenn Jordan directed me in *My Brother's Keeper*, we had lengthy discussions about the distinct characters of the two brothers. [Lithgow played dual roles in the film.] Glenn had prepared a long list of adjectives, one for one brother and one for the other. This pointed out quite clearly how they differed.

My first experience with film was very difficult. The film was Dealing, and when I arrived on the set it was quite busy. No one had the time to explain anything to me, and so I went through the movie trying to pick up on various technical things. With the series, I see the same thing happening with actors who, even though they've had a lot of stage experience, know absolutely nothing about the operation of a film set.

I think one of the most important things I learned was how to be good when you're off camera. When they shoot the other actor's close-ups, you have to know how to help the other actor without expending all of your energy on it.

On *The World According to Garp*, directed by George Roy Hill, we had two weeks of rehearsal. The first week was in a large gymnasium, and we had the sets all taped out on the floor. We actually played the scenes and did run-through of the whole script. The second week we rehearsed on location. The cameraman and the writer were there to help with any problems. So by the time we shot it, we knew what we were going to do. I even rehearsed with a skirt on and tied a scarf around my neck.

Before any of this took place, and quite by accident, I had read a book a couple of years back, a memoir by Jan Morris, who was one of the first trans-sexuals. I know I would have read this book for the role as research, but to tell you the truth I am not an exhaustive researcher.

I decided to play Roberta [the transsexual character] very much how I'd play myself had I undergone a sex change. But I did think a whole lot about the notion of transsexuality as opposed to transvestism—the former being very real and the latter a sort of play acting. The transsexual feels more herself as a woman than a man. With that thought in mind, the growth of the character became organic. I tried to play her as dignified and simple with an inconspicu-ous performance. I'd let the absurdity of the image take care of itself.

I'll tell you a funny story about George Roy Hill. The first shot for Roberta was when she was tied to a tree and the kids were playing knights in shining armor. There I was screaming like a damsel in distress. At the end of the scene I went to George and told him that after all the rehearsal work, I still didn't feel prepared. This insecurity might have been prompted by the fact that after I auditioned for the part, George went on to audition eighty more actors. I asked him if I was hitting the right tone, was I overdoing it? All of the things an insecure actor would conjure up. George bellowed, "I'm glad you brought that up." My heart fell into my stomach and I went pale. And after a beat, he roared with laughter and assured me that he'd let me know if anything was wrong. That was the literally the last thing he said to me through the whole shoot. The work had been done in rehearsal, and now you just did your job. That's all he asked. One day I said to him, "there must be fifteen different things a director has to worry about." He replied there were only three things—the script, the cast, the execution.

The hardest thing about movie making is keeping yourself alive. As I said before, the pace is quite slow. The fact that they shoot the master scene first makes it even more important to know that the coverage, the close-ups, will come later in the day.

Situation Comedy

For me, sitcom acting was a return to theater. You work on the material, you learn your lines, you rehearse, and then you perform. When you shoot in front of a live audience, you're giving them a polished piece of theater. You want them to be entertained. You need their laughter and their energy to inspire you. And very much like theater, you can't screw up. But unlike the theater where you have to keep going, when you screw up on a sitcom you get to do it over again.

One big difference with a TV audience is they can leave if they get bored. You can't repeat a scene so often that the jokes become sour. Basically we have two passes at a scene. Between the first and second take, the writers have to solve whatever didn't work the first time. I forgot to mention that the writers are there for the taping. The sitcom relies on the writers until the show is in the can. You'd think the audience wouldn't laugh the second time because they've heard all the jokes before. But they laugh all the harder because they appreciate the variations.

Sometimes I get into a rhythm and plan two ways of doing a scene. I save what I think is the best way for the second take. The element of surprise really helps for the laughs and also for the cast. Another important thing about sitcom acting is the cast becomes an ensemble. We get to know each other, and through that we play scenes much more effortlessly.

The premise of the show really unleashed all of us. Being aliens, we didn't know what proper behavior was. So as an actor, this gave us a lot of room. We could do wild things, stuff that nobody would accept if we were human beings.

It's probably the most fun I've ever had as an actor. It takes me back to college days when you would just go for it. That's not to say that we throw out certain rules that make theater work. Even with all of the freedom, there have to be definite signposts in the writing that allow you to get from A to B.

An interesting case in point was our Christmas show. There was a scene where I had to change from the bad Scrooge to the good Scrooge. The original script made the transition too quickly and made it impossible to play. I think a basic tenet of acting is you must have a reason to change your mind, and this must be stimulated by some thought or action.

This time we motivated the change by a prop. Nina, the office secretary is so pissed off by my sour Christmas attitude that she bangs down her gift to me on my desk. I growl, "What's this?" and she replies, "It's your Christmas present." I just stare at it for a beat, then she yells, "Go on open it!" So I open it and take out a travel coffee mug. Again I ask her, "What's this?" because as an alien I honestly don't know what it is. Now the mug becomes the focus of my attention, and I am genuinely curious about it. In effect we have softened the anger by my naïveté.

Now Nina has a choice. She can ignore the question and buzz off, or she can answer it. I think Nina answers the question because she realizes that I truly do not know what it is. "It's a travel mug," she says. "It's so you don't spill your coffee in your lap every morning." And I reply, "Oh, you noticed that." Then it dawns on me that this coffee mug is something very useful to me and Nina realized that. I say, "I need this." She starts out of the room and says, "You're welcome."

The mug has effectively begun the transition, and then it's very easy for me to transfer that feeling to Nina. I say, "Forget the work, go to the Christmas party." She asks if I'm sure. That line and her reading of it nurture the change, and by softening her attitude she allows me to go further. I say, "Yes," then, as she leaves, "Nina, Merry Christmas."

The transition is completed. The original scene had none of these stepping stones, and it was my actor's instinct that compelled me to ask for them. The actor needs stepping stones, clues, reasons to effect drastic changes.

The TV sitcom is very much a writers' and actors' medium. The director acts as a referee and more importantly sees to it that the four cameras catch the action when they're supposed to. By the way, the four-camera technique makes it incumbent on the actor to always keep alive. You never know which take they'll use in the edit process, and though the other actors may have that particular moment, they may want to cut to you for a reaction shot.

In both film and television the actor should try to bring something to the project. I think it's a luxury for a director to have actors who have good ideas. The whole thing is a process of taking it seriously and not taking it seriously. I like to have fun with it. Somehow it makes it easier.

However wild you get you should always try to match action. Because if you don't, there's a very good chance the scene won't edit together. The result is you've lost a perfectly wonderful performance because of your technical mistakes.

I believe in a strong technique. Discipline frees one creatively. I like to rehearse, know what I'm going to do, then go on from there. Other actors may not work that way, and that's fine. It really doesn't matter how you get there. It's what you do when you're there that counts.

11

The Workplace

The Set

A movie stage is a small country run by a benevolent, enlightened (we hope) dictator called the director. It is designed for efficiency in making the film and little else. The back of the set faces bare walls with thick soundproof material. Electrical and grip equipment is stored along the edges. It is a large warehouse, an esthetic horror, and not very comfortable.

In the middle of this space is the set or a group of sets. Above it is a grid where large lights are hung. A sound cart with tape recorder and perhaps a few chairs line the perimeter. On a shooting day, the set is always crowded with people performing their various tasks—gaffers, grips, boom operator, property technician, set designer, makeup artist, camera crew, production assistants. All are necessary for the scene that is to be shot.

Let's describe a few of the important jobs that surround the actor. Next in importance to the director is the director of photography, whose responsibility is to light the set and the actors and sometimes to help the director in camera placement. The camera itself is usually handled by two people, the operator and the focus puller. It is wise to stay in their good graces. The boom operator handles the microphone, which usually looms over the actors' heads. You must become aware of this object, because its sudden movements can trigger an unintentional response from the actor. A few feet away from the set is the sound mixer with a tape recorder. In film the sound is recorded separately from the film. What makes the sound mixer happy is an actor who rehearses and performs at the same sound level.

Hovering near the director is the continuity person. One of the many things this person is responsible for is watching the actors' action. The continuity person documents details such as that you held a glass in your left hand while you answered the phone with your right hand. It is not untoward to ask the continuity person for help if you are in doubt.

There are many more people on a set, all doing important jobs, each collaborating to make the film. The last one I'll mention is the assistant director. The assistant director does not help the director direct but helps the director by running the set. It is a pressure-filled job the myriad responsibilities of which require a firm, professional hand. Don't take it personally if the assistant director doesn't inquire about how your day was when you're requested on the set.

In most production centers, jobs are unionized. This means one important thing to the actor. If something on the set has to be moved and it is not during a scene, don't move it. You are there to act and not to be "helpful." By doing anything other than acting, you may be infringing on someone else's job.

In a far corner are a few dressing rooms for the actors. Comfortable but small they are shelters from frenzied activity. The leading players usually have luxurious trailers parked adjacent to the stage. The makeup tables are near the dressing rooms. In some cases you'll go to the makeup building for the first makeup job, then someone will do touch-ups on the set. The number of makeup artists depends on how many actors are on call that day. If there are a large number and the producer wants to save money, you can be sure that your morning call will be very early so that one makeup artist can do several people.

So there you are at 7 A.M., made up and ready to go. Except the schedule says that your scene is at 11 A.M. You know your lines—boy, do you know your lines—and now you try to stop going over them for fear they are going to be stale by the time you say them. You contemplate a catnap, but that might take the edge off. Besides, you can't sleep. You can't take a walk because the schedule might change.

They begin shooting another scene at 9 A.M. It's a scene that appears much later in the script. As you watch, you become aware that the scene involves a character who's in your scene later, and you start to form notions about that character regarding your scene. You then realize these notions are turning into strong ideas, and you begin to picture the scene in your head.

LEAVE! Don't watch. You must be concerned with the other character only as he or she relates to you in the scene you are doing. The fact that movies are shot out of sequence can lead you to form opinions that are not valid.

The champion of champions in the hurry-up-and-wait game is movie making. You have to learn to deal with it. My best suggestion is to do something that occupies your mind in a light-hearted way. Read an easy nonfiction book. Do a crossword puzzle. Play solitaire. Redo your address book. Exercise (without sweating). If you feel it necessary, do all of these things in character. The main thing is to keep the energy flowing and not to get involved.

Some actors don't need any of this. Anthony Hopkins, who played the maniacal Dr. Lecter in *The Silence of the Lambs*, remarked that he was quite able to relax on the set, talk with friends, and generally have a good time, and then, when it came time to shoot, immediately jump into character. Jodie Foster, on the other hand, would do none of that. Jodie Foster was said to be intense on the set and to keep to herself between takes. That may or may not be true, but it illustrates a point. Few actors can turn character on and off at will, jumping from laughs and jokes with friends to performing a dramatic scene.

Let's assume that you are one of those actors who wishes to focus on the work without too many distractions. You've kept active, and now they call you to the set. After greetings, the director asks to run the scene. Being the fine actor you are, you listen carefully to the other character and respond accordingly. After a couple of suggestions the director blocks the scene very loosely. You can be damn sure the director has the blocking already in mind because the set is lit and the camera is placed. Still, you're allowed some creative latitude, and if you can't do a movement gracefully, chances are the director will change it.

At this point, the director of photography probably will want to do some last minute tweaks, and you'll be asked to stand in various key spots so the work can be done. The director of photography may carry a light meter, a small black object, and hold it very close to your face. On an efficient set, this last-minute tweaking of the lighting shouldn't take long, and the assistant director will call for silence and say something like, "We're going for a take!"

If you're normal, the adrenaline will start to surge. The director calls for one last rehearsal and makes minor adjustments. These minor adjustments can range from a simple reminder to the camera operator regarding a movement to, in rare cases, a complete redo of the blocking and the performance.

It is the latter decision that concerns us. I am assuming that at this point you have not done fifteen movies, but even if you have, you should still remember this next sentence. *It is not your fault.*

Actors tend to become paranoid when the scene doesn't work for the director. Think of this—maybe it just doesn't work, and no one is to blame. Keep still, keep quiet, and wait. It may be a movement. It may be a line. Wait for the fix to emanate from the director.

A good director usually huddles with the actors to solicit their opinions. You may speak if you wish. I've observed scenes become entirely different by the simple direction of one actor doing, or not doing, a piece of business or looking or not looking away at a given time. Whatever you do, don't make radical changes on your own. You may have a tendency to try harder. Don't!

The same paranoia develops when there are multiple takes. Never ask the director whether it's your fault. There can be so many reasons for multiple takes, they're impossible to list. When this happens the thing you can do as an actor is make subtle changes in delivery. I emphasize the word *subtle.* This happens naturally if you are listening and reacting to the other character.

It is the action that has to be repeated the same way on each take, not the acting. To do the identical performances time after time reduces you to being a puppet, not to mention a very dull actor. Repeat your performance exactly only when the director requests it.

Look upon the set as a friendly environment. Robert Mitchum remarked in an interview that he had just done a picture with a young actress who was quite nervous. Mitchum pointed out to her that the entire crew was on her side, pulling for her. Unless you go out of your way to earn their animosity, this is quite true. Allow yourself to feel this support. Except on rare occasions, a film crew is one of the most highly skilled groups of people you'll ever meet. The craft demands technical perfection, and all of their skills are dedicated to making the actors look good. Think about it—they wouldn't be there if it weren't for the actors.

The Location

A location shoot is exactly what the name suggests. You go some place away from the studio to make the film. The same rules apply to a location shoot with just a couple of exceptions.

First, if the location is a public place, where people from the area are allowed to watch, the actor must be wary of playing the goodwill ambassador to the detriment of the job. This is especially true on locations away from the environs of Los Angeles and New York—anyplace where films are not usually shot. The distractions can be enormous. The urge to respond to the locals' natural curiosity is insistent. They'll stare, shout, and ask for autographs. It doesn't matter if you have a tiny, tiny part. The fact that you're there with the movie company makes you a celebrity. What do you do? You've been raised to be polite.

These people buy the tickets. They're your audience. The fact is, you don't really have to do anything. When a film goes on location, someone usually is hired to take care of these situations. It could be a location publicist, the production manager, or even an assistant director. The point is, you don't have any responsibility to respond actively.

The best way to deal with local spectators is to manufacture a wonderful smile. Put it on when you leave the dressing room, and lose it when you reach the camera. Don't listen to what the onlookers say, and don't answer. The smile is enough. I might add that sometimes you'll hear a few unflattering remarks regarding your anatomy or your family tree. These comments especially should be ignored. Smile. The funniest question, which I've heard many times, is, "Who are you?" This one, for sure, doesn't deserve an answer.

The only other location danger has to do with your fellow workers. Real bonding occurs on location, a true sense of family and good feelings. The one important thing to keep in mind is that no one cares what the crew looks like the next day. They are not on camera. You are. It's easy to be caught up in fun after a long, hard day of shooting. But a makeup artist can do only so much, and those close-ups can be deadly.

Another note about makeup. Do not try to "improve" the makeup artists' work. They know what they're doing, and you don't. If, by chance, you're on a really low-budget shoot or a student film on which there is no makeup person, remember one thing: Stage makeup technique looks grotesque on camera.

Women should make up for everyday life, time of day being important. The eyes should be natural and the foundation not too pale. Avoid severe lines and shadows. Men with ruddy skin tones usually don't need makeup. The others just need a base to warm up the complexion. Avoid any eye treatment that one can see. In other words, if you look made up, the camera will see it.

Lights, Camera, Action

Good film and television actors must always know where the camera is but never show it. They should also know where the key lights are and the microphone. The idea that the technicians will catch you no matter where you go, what you do, and how soft you whisper is a conceit. Norman Jewison spoke of a very famous actor who purposefully did the scene differently on each take. He never bothered to try to match action. He went so far as to introduce new business when they shot coverage. The consequences were that in the editing process there was very little to choose from because nothing matched. The actor's performance, as good as he is, was limited by his perversity on the set.

The key light catches the actor's expression and is an essential tool of the cinematographer. If you have a small part and in the course of the scene park yourself in front of the star so that your shadow prevents the key light from hitting him or her, chances are you're going to hear, "Cut!" Several key lights are put strategically on the set to catch various moments in the scene. A quick glance during rehearsal tells you how to clear those lights. Sometimes the set is lit without keys. You can usually identify this situation when you see that the lights are not shining directly onto the set but are bounced off white cards. Another way of getting this soft lighting effect is to put diffusion in front of the lamps. Sets or locations lit this way eliminate shadows to a great degree. This makes it easier for the actors to stay out of each other's light.

You may well ask why an actor should worry about such things. The answer is not to worry. Assess the situation, put it in the back of your mind, and act. A good director and director of photography watch for these things in rehearsal and modify either the lights or the blocking to correct them.

What you normally hear after someone yells, "Quiet on the set," is this: a loud bell that tells people outside the set that a take is being shot. Then the assistant director says, "We're going for a take. Roll sound."

SOUND PERSON: "Sound rolling."
ASSISTANT DIRECTOR: "Roll camera."
CAMERA OPERATOR: "Camera rolling."
SOUND TECHNICIAN: "Speed."
ASSISTANT DIRECTOR: "Mark it."
SLATE PERSON: "Scene 32 'Apple' take one."

The person holding the clapboard clicks it shut and leaves. The director says, "action." There may be one slight change. The clapboard person may not say the scene number and just click the board shut. This is because the sound person has already slated the scene at the recorder stand. Don't say any lines until the director says, "action!" or gives some other signal, but while all this is happening, get into the scene. Establish eye contact with the person or people with whom you're doing the scene, and think of what you'd be saying if the scene had started already.

When the scene is finished, the director says, "Cut!" This is very important. Do not stop acting the second you hear, "Cut!" Good camera operators continue to roll for five or ten seconds after they hear, "Cut!" Some of the best reactions happen during those seconds. Wait until the set begins to stir and you sense that the camera is off.

Starting and stopping the camera wastes film. Once the actor understands this and behaves correctly, the producer will be a happy person. To illustrate: You are in close-up for two or three lines. You blow it. You're embarrassed and angry with yourself. Don't move away and leave the scene. Forget it immediately.

Stay in character and start again. One more goof? It's OK. Begin again. You can do three or four takes in this fashion and still use less film had you stopped and lost position, forcing a camera stop. The director may even give you direction while the camera rolls. The camera operator may ask you to tilt your head two or three inches. The important thing is to keep working in character. Even the look when you blow your lines, if it's in character, can be used.

The standard procedure is to shoot a master then shoot coverage—the close-ups. This usually means the set needs some preparation. Lights have to be moved, for example. This can take from ten minutes to half and hour and even more. Your task is to remember which take or takes the director chose to be printed and what your performance was on those takes.

A brief technical note: On multiple takes, the director makes a decision to print one, two, or maybe three versions. Because printing the film is expensive, the director makes this limited selection in order to watch the chosen takes the next day. This viewing is called *watching the dailies*. On budget-minded television movies, the director tries to limit the number of takes to one or two. In this case both usually are printed.

Back to your coverage. The setup time is past, and you are ready to do the scene again, this time in close-up. Again, you are allowed to make subtle changes. This time, however, with the camera so close, you must be wary of making large moves. After your coverage, the camera is reversed, and you do the scene once again for the other actor's close-up.

Say this is the only scene scheduled for you that day, and the call sheet says the other scene is tomorrow. The crew is setting up on another set.

Do not leave.
Do not get out of costume.
Go to your dressing room and wait.

Either the assistant director or a production assistant will come and release you. They'll also remind you of your next call, hand you a call sheet with the information on it, and confirm that you understand. By the way, during the work day, whenever you leave the set, no matter how short a time, always tell the assistant director or production assistant exactly where you are going.

Sound

Modern technology has given the sound technician many new tools to capture what the actors say. These sensitive instruments also record every other sound on the set. This means the actor must be careful not to handle props in such a way that would cover dialogue. The keys you put on the table make quite a racket. If there is no dialogue, the sound editor can soften that racket easily. But if you happen to talk as you put the keys down, you may cover the line so that it is unusable.

Chairs squeak. Newspapers rustle. Ice cubes in glasses rattle. Actors must be aware of these noises and do their best to speak around them. The fact that objects hardly seem to you to make any noise is deceiving. Remember that the microphone amplifies sound.

Most of the time in a scene between two actors, the sound technician uses one microphone. The boom operator (the one who holds the mike on a large pole) switches back and forth as each actor speaks. The use of one mike means that both voices are being recorded on one channel. If one actor speaks in whispers and the other in a normal voice, it is necessary for the sound mixer to quickly adjust the volume so each is recorded at nearly the same level. An aware film actor tries to match the volume of the other actor doing the scene.

There's some license in this, so you don't have to worry about being absolutely accurate. It is only when the difference is extreme that impossible sound problems occur. It is these impossible sound problems that make it necessary for actors to loop.

ADR: Looping

Automatic dialogue replacement (ADR or *looping*) is the method of recording lines of dialogue that for technical reasons cannot be recorded during shooting. Looping also is used when the director is not satisfied with a line reading and wishes to get another interpretation.

Because so many films nowadays are shot on location, looping has become a large part of production. Bob Baron, the ADR mixer at Paramount Pictures estimates that forty to ninety percent of dialogue is looped. In an interview, Baron gave me the following tips for actors.

ADR stages are recording studios. This means they are usually sterile environments with dead sound. The microphones are set up in front of a large movie screen. The film is cut so the actors see only the portion they are to work on, usually one or two lines at a time.

Sound technicians play the lines to be replaced so you can get an idea of the rhythm. Listen carefully. On the next rehearsal mouth the lines while listening to yourself on the screen. At this point, the director may make suggestions for interpretation, and the mixer asks for a voice check.

There are times on a set when you say your lines without the words being recorded. This is called MOS, which stands for *mit out sound*. This phrase came about years ago when a German director, using the word for *with* in his native language, called for takes without sound. The term came to be used throughout the industry. Back to ADR.

When it's time for a take, this is what happens. The picture comes on the screen, usually a few seconds before your line. You hear three quick beeps just before you are to speak. These beeps are rhythmically placed. Feel the rhythm, and begin your dialogue when the logical fourth beep would come. On paper it would appear:

Beep . . . Beep . . . Beep . . . Dialogue

The most common mistake is to come in too soon after the third beep. Think of the beeps as a musical introduction.

It's important to know that the sound track has been cleared of all extraneous sounds so that your voice is the only thing you hear (unless another actor has an interjection). Because of this, you'll feel quite naked, and the tendency is to pull back. Don't. If anything, the mixer wants more voice, more emotion.

Quite a bit of ADR takes place because a great deal of shooting is done at noisy exteriors. Cars honking, planes overhead, a city bus at the corner all conspire to bury your lines. When you listen to the track during ADR, you don't hear any of this general noise. It is added later. But you must remember that it exists when you redo your lines. That means you use more breath, more volume than you think you need, because when you played the scene on the street you heard the clamor and tried to rise above it.

Even if you're in the distance, keep the level up. The mixer can create the proper perspectives when all the elements are there in the final mix. If you try to create the perspective as you record, you make it more difficult.

Most actors agree that laughing and crying are the most difficult looping assignments. There you are on this modern sound stage watching something you did perhaps a month ago, and the person on the screen—you—is physically carrying on. You're either laughing hysterically or sobbing your heart out. On the stage there's no other actor to play against, and you have to recapture the mood. It's like being at a party and having someone say, "Be funny," or, "Act."

Yes, it's difficult and a lot of actors hate it. But it is a necessary ingredient in the process and must be done. If you accept this and understand the technical process, ADR can be a very creative process. Most important for the actor is to realize that all of the other elements, such as ambient sound and music, are added later. Keep that in mind for your performance. That naked solo voice you hear is not the way the film will sound.

An excellent way to practice ADR is lip-synching. Learn one of your favorite songs, and tape yourself lip-synching it. Play it back while someone videotapes you singing along. It would be wise to pick a song that makes more use of the language than "oh, oh, baby."

Outside Elements

Movie sets and locations attract a lot of activity. Publicity people bring in the press for interviews. The front office has a tour for money people. The various actors' agents show up. Friends and relatives gawk from the perimeter. During breaks, people eat, talk, conduct other business, and tell jokes.

It is not a serene environment. If you wish serenity, make your spot inviolate. If you have a dressing room, go there. If not, do the best you can. Making a movie involves a lot of people doing a lot of jobs. Accept that, and you'll be happy. The fact that you have to cry your heart out in ten minutes because your dog was killed, and it's near the end of the day, and you know you're not going to get more than two takes doesn't make a damn bit of difference. It isn't going to change.

Directors' Peeves

The *New York Times* published an article that listed some of the distractions mentioned earlier. I thought it would be interesting to read directors' views. The main peeve was visitors, especially visitors who engage the actors in business—people like agents, publicity people, and business managers. Relatives and friends ran a close second. Lose the urge to be hospitable; show up for work alone.

Michael Hoffman, the director of *One Fine Day*, starring George Clooney and Michelle Pfeiffer, mentioned actors who are convinced they are "ill." They have a constant anxiety about bacteria. It's a kind of stalling actors use to face up to the fact that they have to go to work and that eventually the work is going to be evaluated by a lot of people. The lesson here is to recognize that your slight physical discomforts are quite normal. Let them run their course and don't panic. A few deep breaths, a moment of relaxation, and you'll manage the butterflies.

Wes Craven, the renowned director of horror films, mentioned the actress who would take off her makeup and redo herself. She'd then claim she hadn't changed a thing. Craven added that just as vexing are cast members who radically change their body shape halfway through a shoot.

On each set there is a large table laden with food for most of the day. Along with the fruit, there are doughnuts, potato chips, candy bars, and soft drinks. Movie crews work long, hard hours, and it's important they know the table is really for them. It doesn't matter if they gain a pound or two. For actors, however, it can mean popping buttons in a very short time. Stay away!

Several directors mentioned actors who forget their lines. This lack of concentration is a lack of courtesy and respect for the other actors. It is time consuming, unprofessional, and unnecessary.

The on-set flirtation or love affair becomes a peeve when the participants decide to break up, become jealous, or have lovers' quarrels. Although some stars may carry on this way, you should forget this part of your nature while working. There may be some very attractive people on the set (it goes with the business), but don't look upon your work as an opportunity to improve your love life.

A movie set is a highly complex organism. Besides the artistic and emotional atmosphere, many complicated technical and mechanical aspects demand the utmost concentration. The fewer the distractions, the better the set runs. Don't make waves. Asking too many questions, not being ready, being in places where you have no business, making silly, minute complaints—any one of these can be the proverbial straw.

12

Scenes

There are numerous books with scenes from plays and movies. For this book, with a couple of exceptions, I have used only original material so that you can't compare yourself with the original performer. In some of my acting and directing classes, in which we used scenes from produced movies, one actress would study the movie scene so thoroughly that she would always bring in a carbon-copy performance. When I asked her not to do this, she replied that the actresses she copied were so much better than she. Her theory was to emulate them on the chance that something would rub off in the process.

Acting, as you know by now, has nothing to do with that kind of behavior. So to prevent emulation, I have written original scenes. The literary merit of the material doesn't matter. The fact that you don't know how the scene fits into the larger whole also is irrelevant. Make the scene a world unto itself. I hope the material suggests specific conflicts, subtexts, and goals. Feel free to extend, change, and invent with only one admonition: don't change the dialogue.

When you audition for a television or movie part, you will receive the same amount of material. You may receive a brief explanation of where the scene fits in, but don't expect to read the whole script. Do the best with what you have.

This is a time to experiment, have fun, and make unusual choices if you wish.

SCENE 1: THE LANGUAGE BARRIER

ONE, who doesn't speak English, has been sent to an office. TWO greets ONE as ONE enters.

TWO

Hi ... I'll be with you in a minute.

TWO completes some work while ONE smiles and waits. After a short time, TWO approaches.

                    TWO
          Have you come about the job?

ONE hands TWO a piece of paper. TWO reads.

                    TWO
          You don't speak much English.

                    ONE
          Yes.

                    TWO
          You do speak English?

                    ONE
          Yes.

                    TWO
          Well that's good. What about word
          processing?

                    ONE
          Yes.

                    TWO
          Excellent.

                    TWO
          The job requires a lot of word
          processing. Are you familiar with
          Microsoft Word?

                    ONE
          Yes.

                    TWO
          Which version?

                    ONE
          Yes.

                    TWO
          Excuse me?

                    ONE
          Yes.

                    TWO
          Uh . . . Are you Stalin's illegitimate
          heir?

                    ONE
          Yes.

                    TWO
          Do you know any other words in
          English?

                ONE AND TWO
          Yes.

TWO now speaks slowly and louder as if that would help the
person understand.

                    TWO
          This job requires someone who speaks
          English . . . English! You don't speak
          English. No . . . speak . . . English. . . .

ONE smiles at TWO.

                    TWO
          NO ENGLISH!

                    ONE
          Yes!

                    TWO
          Not yes . . . No.

                    ONE
          Yes.

                    TWO
          NO! . . . NO! NO! NO!

                    ONE
          No?

TWO is relieved and hands the paper back.

                    TWO
          Good-bye and good luck. I have a lot
          of work to do . . . so thank you.

ONE hands TWO the paper again.

>   TWO
> No. You take.

TWO tries to hand it back, but ONE refuses to take it.

>   TWO
> You take! Please . . .

TWO struggles to get it back into ONE'S hand.

>   TWO
> This is exhausting.

Finally ONE takes the paper and gestures for TWO to read it.
TWO tries to comprehend.

>   TWO
> Look . . . The job requires . . . Why am I
> saying this?

>   ONE
> Macka . . . Macka.

ONE grabs TWO's neck and pulls TWO's head toward the paper.

>   TWO
> I'm going to have to call someone.

>   ONE
> Macka!

ONE gestures from eyes to paper.

>   TWO
> Macka? What? Read?

TWO begins to read the paper and suddenly stops, looks at ONE,
then back to the paper. ONE lets go as TWO straightens up to
read. The paper slowly comes down as TWO looks intently at
ONE. ONE realizes that TWO is understanding. TWO goes to the
desk, takes out an old milk carton, then comes back to ONE. TWO
looks at the picture on the carton, then at ONE.

>   TWO
> Sister [or Brother]!

They embrace.

                                        END OF SCENE

Yes, One has all the good lines. The scene relies on the sincerity of One and the polite frustration of Two. At the end, at the moment of realization before Two goes to get the milk carton, the scene can be played most seriously. This sets up the payoff.

The business with the paper and One's physical move compelling Two to read it must be carefully worked out. The neck business should not be too aggressive; it should be annoying but not alarming. Passing the paper back and forth should be choreographed so that it happens on certain lines each time.

SCENE 2: COLLEGE BOYS

ONE and TWO are roommates. They have just come back from summer break, and they are unpacking their things. The business must have a pattern, and you must adhere to it each take. The actors inventory the items and know the order and where they go.

ONE
So . . . how did it go?

TWO
Great.

ONE
I had to work for my Dad for three weeks, but then I went to New York for a week.

TWO
You didn't even call.

ONE
I did too. They said you were in Kansas.

TWO
Oh yeah . . . that was the week my Grandfather died. Damn, I wished I'd been there. I could have showed you around.

ONE
It would have been nice.

TWO
So what did you do, besides getting
drunk?

ONE
Things.

TWO
Things? You act like you get to New
York every month. So what did you
do? Visit the Empire State? The
Statue of Liberty?

ONE
I went to the Guggenheim art
museum.

TWO
What?

ONE
And I went to see a symphony
concert.

TWO
You went to a symphony concert?

ONE
I was going to go to the opera, but
they were shut down.

TWO
They do shut down in August.

ONE
So instead we went to see a play.

TWO
We? Did I hear you say we?

ONE
Oh . . . didn't I tell you? I met
someone.

TWO
You didn't just meet someone. You
met a sorceress . . . maybe a witch.

                         ONE
Look out!

                         TWO
You're the one who should look out.
Art museums ... symphonies ... Man,
you have been transformed ...
Mutated!

                         ONE
What are you getting so excited
about? You have been trying to get
me to do that stuff for two years.

                         TWO
You're right. Guess I wasn't pretty
enough ...

                         ONE
That's for sure ... So ... what about
you?

                         TWO
Me? I just wasted my time going to
museums, symphonies ... plays ...
same old shit ... except, I met someone too.

                         ONE
That's great.

                         TWO
Remember Harold from down the
hall?

                         ONE
Yeah.

                         TWO
He was always bragging about his
sister.

                         ONE
Eunice.

                         TWO
Hey, you remembered her name. I'm
amazed.

ONE
I'm afraid you will be.

TWO
What makes you say that?

TWO begins to put it together. They each reach into their cases and pull out a framed portrait of Eunice.

ONE AND TWO
We're engaged.

END OF SCENE

SCENE 3: TWO WOMEN

TWO
I told him that I had decided to
become celibate.

ONE
What did he say?

TWO
He asked me what I meant by that. I
explained it to him.

ONE
And he took it like a man.

TWO
In a way. He said we should have one
for the road.

ONE
You were in the car again?

TWO
It's an expression. Remember the
song that old guy used to sing?

ONE
Julio something or other?

                    TWO
No . . . an American. Anyway I said
no.

                    ONE
You're a very principled woman.

                    TWO
I want an uncluttered life with unclut-
tered relationships where I know that
I am liked or disliked for what I am.
Besides, I think I'll have more time to
study.

                    ONE
You'll get straight As and be a
nervous wreck. Personally, I'll settle
for C-pluses if you get what I mean.

                    TWO
I didn't expect you to do it just
because I did.

                    ONE
What a relief.

                    TWO
I know it's an important means of
expression for you.

                    ONE
It makes me want to sing and tap
dance. . . . What do you mean, an
important means of expression?

                    TWO
It fulfills you.

                    ONE
How do you know what it does to
me?

                    TWO
You told me so.

ONE
I have never said the word fulfill in
my life. You know what you're fulfill
of.

TWO
I knew if I told you that you'd have
some sort of jealous fit.

ONE
Jealous of what? Some twit who's had
three . . . no, make that two and a
half ten-second bouts in the back seat
of a Toyota with a man who doesn't
know the meaning of celibate.

TWO
It was a full three.

ONE
You said somebody walked by.

TWO
They did . . . but it was consummated.

ONE
Consummated? You've been consummated? I didn't know. You poor
dear . . . No wonder you're giving it
up.

ONE begins to laugh. TWO doesn't want to, but she soon joins in.
They both ad-lib with the word consummated as a theme.

END OF SCENE

SCENE 4: MAN OR WOMAN

This scene without obvious content is an acting challenge. The words are
not at all what the scene is about. Create your own subtext, do the scene, and
when you view it, ask the group what they thought your subtext was. Did their
views match yours?

                    HE

Hi.

                    SHE

Hi.

                    HE

Did you have a good time?

                    SHE

Not really.

                    HE

Where's your coat?

                    SHE

I didn't take one.

                    HE

I could have sworn you took your
coat.

                    SHE

I didn't need it.

                    HE

Weren't you cold?

                    SHE

No ... Well, the air conditioning was a
bit chilly.

                    HE

It isn't air conditioned.

                    SHE

It most certainly is.

                    HE

That must be new.

                    SHE

It was there from the start.

                    HE

They never used it when I was there.

                    SHE
Perhaps you were there in the
winter?

                    HE
It was spring . . . I was there once in
June . . . But it was a cold damp June.

                    SHE
They often are.

                    HE
Yes.

                    SHE
Not like now.

                    HE
So you wished you had taken your
coat?

                    SHE
I suppose.

                    HE
It always seems that when you take
your coat, you never need it. Then,
when you take it, it's . . .

                    SHE
Hot.

                    HE
Yeah.

                    SHE
I don't think you should say that's
always true.

                    HE
I didn't mean always.

                    SHE
That's what you said.

                    HE
People always say always, but they
really don't mean it.

SHE
I don't. I mean I don't say always.

HE
OK. You don't.

SHE
When I say always, I mean it. That's
why you'll seldom hear me say
always.

HE
You don't like . . . small talk.

SHE
No.

HE
I could tell.

SHE
I suppose.

HE
No supposing about it.

A long pause.

SHE
It was damn cold in there.

_____

END OF SCENE
_____

You might experiment with this scene by choosing a specific locale, situation, or costume, then make a drastic change of these elements on a second take.

_____

THE COMEDY SKETCH: CASA BLANCO

Exterior: an airport.

Bogart and Bergman, a.k.a. Ricky and Ilsa, are about to say good-bye in the moody mist. Ricky is world weary, tough, and taciturn. Ilsa has the accent of a maître d' in a bad continental restaurant.

RICKY
OK baby, you're getting on that plane
and that's that.

ILSA
Oh, Wicky, Wicky, Wicky.

RICKY
That's Ricky, Ricky, Ricky.

ILSA
I just said that.

RICKY
You said, Wicky, Wicky, Wicky.

ILSA
Wight!

RICKY
Wong . . . I mean wrong! It's Ricky
with an R. Not Wicky with a W!

ILSA
Honey, don't be angwy. I want to
stay with you. I love you.

RICKY
Your place is with your husband. He
needs you.

ILSA
I don't love Wictor.

RICKY
That's Victor!

ILSA
Wight! Why do you repeat evewy
thing I say?

RICKY
Forget it.

ILSA
This may be the last time we see
each other.

RICKY

I know . . . But we have our memories
and our special song. (Hums tuneless
melody.) Da dee da da dee da.

ILSA

What's Da dee da da dee da?

RICKY

I forgot the words.

ILSA

You forgot the tune. You forgot the
words to our song? How could you do
such a thing?

Rick continues to sing the same two lines over, trying to
remember. She continues on through this, and he sings louder.

ILSA

You swore you'd never forget it. You
sang it to me after we made love the
first time. We danced to it on the
night we parted. You made a hit
record of it! WILL YOU SHUT UP?

RICKY

I think I've got it! (sings) Twinkle,
twinkle, little . . . little . . .

ILSA

Little jerk.

The roar of the airplane engine.

ILSA

Thank goodness.

PA VOICE

Flight 202 leaving for Lisbon.

RICKY

This is it, baby.

ILSA

Take singing lessons while I'm gone.
And maybe a memowy course.

> RICKY
> What's a memowy course?

> ILSA
> Forget it . . . Maybe you're wight.
> Wictor needs me. Fwance needs me.
> Good-bye Wicky.

She kisses him on the cheek and leaves.

> RICKY
> That's Ricky. (To himself) What's that
> dumb song.

> PA VOICE
> (Sings)
> Twinkle, twinkle, little star.

Rick reacts.

> RICK AND PA VOICE
> (Sing)
> How I wonder what you are.

> RICKY
> Here's looking at you kid!

END OF SCENE

If several couples do this scene, it would be best to tape it without an audience. Withhold playback until all of the versions have been taped. The jokes will get stale, but you should overlook that and watch for technique. Once again, the actors must play it straight and let the humor evolve from characterization. Don't play to the jokes.

SCENE 5: FLIRTATION

ONE approaches TWO, who is reading a bus timetable.

> ONE
> Do you know what time the crosstown
> gets here?

>   TWO
>   No.

>   ONE
>   Is that a timetable?

No answer.

>   ONE
>   A bus timetable?

TWO closes the timetable and turns away.

>   ONE
>   It looked like a bus timetable. That's
>   why I asked. I'd like to borrow it for
>   a second.

TWO waits a beat then hands ONE the schedule. ONE reads it for
a beat.

>   ONE
>   Oh my God! Damn!

>   TWO
>   What?

>   ONE
>   No crosstown till next Thursday.

>   TWO
>   What? Gimme that!

TWO snatches the timetable back and starts to read, then
suddenly stops.

>   TWO
>   Funny . . . very funny.

>   ONE
>   That's two days away . . . we have
>   time for some coffee . . . maybe
>   dinner . . . Breakfast?

>   TWO
>   OK, I give up. . . . The bus will be here
>   in two minutes. Let's try to have an
>   innocuous conversation without

getting cute or personal. I'll start off.
Nice weather we're having .... No,
cancel that ... Have you seen any
good movies lately? ... No ... that can
get deep and philosophical ... and
revealing.... Let me think ... What
about sports? No ... I can't talk about
sports.... I got it! (Breath) How
about Madonna? Let's talk about
Madonna.... You start.

ONE is still bug-eyed at the speech.

> TWO
>
> You've heard of Madonna ...

> ONE
>
> Yes.

> TWO
>
> Not the one who was Jesus's mother.

> ONE
>
> The singer Madonna.

> TWO
>
> Or actress.

> ONE
>
> Either one.

A very long pause.

> ONE
>
> I ... I just wanted to borrow your
> timetable. I didn't mean anything
> else.

> TWO
>
> Sure.

> ONE
>
> I mean it ... Honest ...

> TWO
>
> OK ... I may have overreacted. I'm a
> little edgy. I just lost my job.

                         ONE
            That's funny. I did too.

                         TWO
            No kidding.

The bus comes and they stand there. The bus leaves.

                         TWO
            Now you've made me miss my bus.

                         ONE
            It was my bus too.

                         TWO
            We could walk.

TWO takes a step and stops when ONE doesn't follow.

                         TWO
            Well . . . come on.

                         ONE
            I have to tell you something.

                         TWO
            Go on.

                         ONE
            I just said I lost my job because you
            said you lost yours. . . . I don't work.

TWO smiles.

                         TWO
            Neither do I. . . . I just said I lost my
            job as an excuse . . .

TWO nods a come-along and walks off. ONE follows.

                                        END OF SCENE

EXERCISE 24: SACRIFICE

ONE reads a note. TWO knows what's to come, but tries to ignore it.

> ONE
> The job came through.

> TWO
> I knew it would. So . . . are you going?

> ONE
> I'll never get another chance like this.

> TWO
> You have to take it.

> ONE
> What about you? I can't leave you
> here.

> TWO
> I can visit. Look, we both know
> you're going to take it. We've been
> apart before.

> ONE
> But not for this long. . . . It's two
> thousand miles from here. It's not
> like you can drive over on the week-
> end.

> TWO
> Let's not go over all the negatives.

> ONE
> You really want me to take the job?

> TWO
> Yes.

> ONE
> Because if you say no, I won't.

> TWO
> I really want you to take the job.

```
                              ONE
          OK. Then I will.

                              TWO
          Good.
```

TWO turns away. ONE waits a beat, then leaves.

EXERCISE 25: DISCOVERY

You are desperate. The room contains something, some bit of evidence that's vital to save your lover's life. The search reveals nothing. You are defeated. Then, inspiration, you think of a place, go to it, and find what you've been looking for.

                                                    END OF SCENE

This scene should be shot in a long master, then broken up into coverage. The close-ups should be story points, such as defeat, then inspiration.

For further study, take scenes from plays rather than films and tape them with film techniques. With respect to the authors and only for the purpose of exercise, you should cut the dialogue to a minimum. In other words, make them film scenes. This is a good opportunity to perform the scenes with a play version and a film version. In each version, the acting should be the same. But in the film version, make modifications to accommodate the camera and sound, as with close-ups and reaction shots.

13

The Business

Film and television production costs money. Lots of money. It is not a misnomer when they call it the motion picture *industry*. On one side you have the creative elements and on the other, the business people. In between lies a small battleground. I say small, because there is an awareness on both sides of what the problems are and an accommodation because of them.

The actor plays an important role in this real-life drama. When one reads about the excesses of the movie business, the finger is usually pointed at directors. But actors also have their share. It is a small community, and one can get an unsavory reputation very quickly.

The rumor mill on actors usually mentions one or all of the following complaints. The actor is (1) unprepared, (2) incompetent, or (3) difficult. Actors should be especially wary of being labeled difficult. A movie production is a complex organization in which many skilled and creative people deal with both high technology and artistic expression. It is an ideal spot for Murphy's Law.

Murphy's Law is that anything that can go wrong will go wrong. Through no fault of yours, you may be thrust onto a set where Murphy's Law has struck with a vengeance. You finally get to do your four lines, and you are great. Then a small voice announces that the camera jammed and none of the footage is usable. They then announce lunch, and you have to wait.

After lunch you prepare to redo the scene, and the producer insists the lines aren't right. The director and producer huddle together, each throwing lines to try and fix the scene. The result is a hodgepodge of what you did before, without the finesse.

You work on the new lines, and it's time for a take. Halfway through, the director yells, "Cut!" and huddles with the producer; you feel their eyes on you. You know they're thinking it isn't the dialogue, it's the actor. But you're wrong. Another change, a brief rehearsal, and they're ready to shoot again. You get a lot of encouragement and praise and are ready to emote. Halfway through, a large jet flies over at four hundred feet.

Let's face it. You have every right to be thoroughly upset. As Archie Bunker would say on "All in the Family," *Stifle it.*

If you expect and prepare for Murphy's Law, you can face these difficulties with equanimity. If you add to the chaos by making a scene, it will be duly noted, and even though the circumstances warrant some reaction, all that will be remembered is your outburst.

Other actors who are called difficult are never satisfied with their performances and insist on doing more takes. You can politely ask for one more every so often, but to insist on it after the director wishes to move on is a definite breach of professional etiquette.

By the way, the Murphy's Law for actors is this—Nothing bad happens when you are mediocre. It's only when everything seems to click for you that things go wrong.

You learn to work with a director and work around certain aspects so he can hear your point of view. You don't get angry. You don't go crazy. If a director wants something from you, you find a way to get there, to work around it.

Samuel L. Jackson

To sum it up, you can be absolutely right and very, very wrong.

Agents

You can't get a job without an agent, and you can't get an agent without a job. You'll hear this Catch-22 situation all the time. The fact is, you can get an agent without a job, but it takes real work, persistence, and the proper materials. The Screen Actors Guild (SAG) publishes a list of agents, as do several private companies. Some of them designate whether they see new people.

The proper materials are:

1. A one-page resume that lists your educational and acting experience. Do not list extraneous jobs that have nothing to do with the business.
2. A couple of good head shots (photographs). If you submit glamour shots, also include a shot that just looks like you. Many times I have been handed photographs by actors who bear no resemblance to their pictures. Pictures should be recent. Even though you think you haven't changed that much, using five-year-old pictures can have a detrimental effect on casting directors.

The hard work and persistence have to do with not being discouraged and keeping a positive attitude. You must believe that someday something will happen. There are stories of famous actors who persevered for years until they got their "break."

One of the better ways to get an agent is to join an actor's showcase. These are studios where actors, for a fee, attend workshops and every so often do scenes for invited guests. Agents and casting directors check out these showcases quite often.

Join a little-theater group. Don't worry if the other actors are doing it for a hobby. And don't give the impression that just because you intend to become a professional, the work is child's play. Many amateur actors are quite good but have chosen not to make it their livelihood. Whatever the venue, little theater, trade show, local commercial theater, it's vital to give one hundred percent. You never know who's watching. The important thing is to make as many contacts as you can.

Should you move to Los Angeles or New York? It depends on what you want. There are many opportunities to do stage work in both places. You might want that extra year of honing your craft. Because Los Angeles has more film and television work, it may offer a better prospect of being discovered. Both places are filled with people just like you, all looking for work.

My advice for the recent college graduate or ambitious amateur is to go somewhere and do regional theater for a year or so. If there's a film school nearby, try to do student films and videos.

For employment, I suggest a job that offers time flexibility. Waiting on tables is a good example. It is easy to get someone to cover for you if an interview comes up. It seems as if half of the table servers in New York are actors.

Auditions and Casting

Jane Feinberg, formerly a partner in Fenton and Feinberg, one of the best casting firms in Los Angeles, supplied the following information about casting. Her firm's credits include *Raiders of the Lost Ark, ET: The Extraterrestrial, Godfather II,* and *One Flew Over the Cuckoo's Nest* among many movies and television shows.

Because of her or his expertise in finding the right people for all the parts in a film, a casting director is hired by the producer during preproduction. Sometimes the project is already attached to a star, but when it isn't, the casting director formulates casting ideas from the stars down to the player who has one line.

After reading the script, the casting director lists the parts and the types to fill them. This list is discussed with the producer and the director, and, after consensus is reached, the casting director sends sheets to agents telling them what types of actors the movie requires. The agents set up meetings for their clients, hoping to fulfill those requirements. The casting director meets those actors and chooses who will meet or audition for the director and producer.

In general this procedure is predicated on the fact that actors have agents and are members of SAG. What about actors without agents and no union membership? How do they get into this mechanism?

Besides casting specific projects, casting directors are looking for fresh and interesting actors to add to their casting lists. They go to local plays, showcases, and workshops for that purpose. They also listen to friends who recommend people. In Los Angeles and New York is a company called Breakdown Services, which lists most of the open casting calls for every imaginable type of show. This list goes out to managers and agents. Even if an agent doesn't represent you, you might talk one into giving you access to the list.

To meet new actors, agents and casting directors may invite them to a general interview. These short sessions are very important for actors, and some dos and don'ts apply. Because this kind of meeting is nonspecific in that you just chat and aren't auditioning for a part, it is difficult give advice on achieving good results. Why do two people like each other instantly and two others don't? You are there on a semispiritual plane, hoping your two psyches meld. Let's get to the *don'ts* to help improve the odds.

Don't think you have to be charming, witty, blasé, worldly, diffident, sophisticated, smart, chic, flippant, rude, obsequious, smarmy, or cute.

Don't dress up or down; don't wear a bizarre creation from a weird designer or the remnants of your sixties-looking wardrobe.

Don't bring in every picture taken of you since birth or clippings showing each and every time your name has been in print.

Don't be late, make excuses, or take charge.

Don't lie.

Now for the dos.

Do be yourself!

Do give evidence of your training and your serious intent to be an actor. Be enthusiastic and focused. If you're asked to read a line for a small part, do it naturally, honestly. Don't try to make this one line the summation of all your previous training.

Do leave your picture (the one that looks like you) and a brief résumé. On the résumé, include only items that relate directly to acting. General interests and skills are fine, but detailed information about your hobbies is irrelevant.

Let's examine an actual audition for a part. The odds are pretty slim that you'll get the part. You're turned down approximately twenty-nine times out of thirty. The sessions last only a few minutes. Often as soon as you walk in the door, you're automatically rejected for some physical reason, such as being too short, having the wrong hair color, or being the wrong age or weight. There are too many reasons to mention. But still you must try.

Some actors try to look the part, dress as the character, and affect mannerisms. A story was printed in the *New York Times* about an actress named Mary Carver. When she appeared to audition for the part of an insane woman in *I Never Promised You A Rose Garden*, Ms. Carver handed the casting director a note that said, "My name is Mary Carver. Don't talk to me." Abruptly Ms. Carver began singing "On the Good Ship Lollipop" while brushing her hair. She swore at a passerby, who turned out to be the producer, and in general made the filmmakers, including a specialist in mental illness, so nervous that they ordered her ejected onto Hollywood Boulevard. At this point, Ms. Carver broke character, and got the job.

This is an extreme way to go and most of the time is quite unnecessary. I'll leave it to you to make the decision when to do it all in character, but do it rarely. Casting directors report being choked, struck, and passionately kissed by actors going too far. Word gets around if you try the trick too often; you become known not as an actor but as a nut.

Unemployment and Rejection

If one word were to guarantee your success in this highly competitive business, it would not be *talent* or *luck*—it would be *persistence*. An actor who sets goals and never stops working toward them almost always gets work. You cannot wait around and hope something will happen.

Instead you go to workshops, classes, and showcases and read the trade papers and casting sheets. You work at conventions as a greeter or handing out samples. You expand your social circles and purposely, without becoming obnoxious, let people know what you do. Better yet, you have a rich relative who buys a studio. Lacking such a relative, find out if friends of friends, friends of relatives, old college pals of your father or mother, any contacts you can think of have any connection whatsoever with the film or television business. Look up these contacts and let them know what you do. These may be long shots, but they could land you an acting job.

Harrison Ford was asked in an interview who discovered him. He replied, "I suppose if I had to say that someone discovered me, it would be a composer in Laguna Beach, Ian Bernard." The fact is, Harry Ford, as he was then known, and I were doing a play together. I thought he was talented and sent him to meet a casting director I knew at Columbia Pictures. To tell you the truth, I had forgotten about it and was quite surprised when he mentioned it years later.

The fact is, you don't know where your break is coming from, so you'd better be ready, because you usually get only one chance.

Be prepared.

14

This Is a Wrap!

In the course of writing this book, I talked to a few actors and directors who said, "Acting is acting," or "I just do what I do." These Zen-like statements have little relevance to student actors. In fact, they don't make sense. Very good actors would say this to me, and when I attempted to question them further, they would fall silent. I respected their feelings, but it made me wonder why they think that way.

I believe those words say something else about the person. The fact is, they don't know what they do and they don't care to examine the process in an intellectual manner. The muse is so fragile to them, they're afraid if they speak of technique, or even think about it, their creative juices will dry up. They're like the country guitar player who sets up the strings incorrectly and uses weird fingering but still plays incredibly well. The guitar player says, "Nobody learnt me different."

Other actors interviewed thought about the question of stage versus film acting and at first denied any difference. But as questions arose, they realized they had many modifications in technique, almost commonsense modifications. When you know the sensitivity of a microphone and its ability to pick up the slightest whisper, you are given a new acting tool. When you know the camera can focus on your eyes to see the smallest tear or hint of emotion, you realize how little you have to do to communicate.

Stage-trained actors with all the basic tools should have no trouble with these modifications. Once they are aware of the possibilities of the camera, perfection of technique should be easy. Not so the other way around.

When a famous movie actress made her stage debut in a Broadway play, the critic for the New York Times suggested the actress had "internalized too much."

The word internalized could be the key to the difference between stage technique and film technique. During stage performances, the audience is a participant in the process. The actor plays a certain way in response to that. You might say the actor reaches out to the audience. In film, the camera, an inanimate device, plays no part in the drama; the actor knows that feedback will come only from the director after the take. During the performance, it is only you, the other actors, and the camera. Good film actors know that the close-up lens allows them to internalize and that the most subtle nuance will be captured.

The actor who believes the only difference between stage acting and film acting is "making it smaller" for film is missing opportunities to create a new technique. The actress mentioned earlier who internalized too much for the stage is an excellent film performer who is much in demand. In fact, she's a star. She is also proof that one can excel in film without stage training.

> *Actors are very delicate instruments. In order for them to do their work, they have to, to some degree, expose areas of themselves that are terribly personal. There are 35 to 65 people around you on the set. . . . At least two thirds of those people are going to be watching the actor do his work. So the ego is forever exposed.*
>
> *Sidney Poitier*

I hope this book has helped some of those wonderful egos and made you realize that for every actor from bit player to star, the experience is much the same. Film and television acting is a demanding profession, one that takes talent and careful study.

You may rely on your talent to surpass expectations, but rely on your technique to fulfill them.

I leave you with one thought about film and television acting: Nothing is forever. But once you've committed a performance to film, it will seem like it.

Index

Lightning Source UK Ltd.
Milton Keynes UK
08 June 2010

155278UK00001B/89/P